Hadoop Cluster Deployment

Construct a modern Hadoop data platform effortlessly and gain insights into how to manage clusters efficiently

Danil Zburivsky

BIRMINGHAM - MUMBAI

Hadoop Cluster Deployment

First published: November 2013

Production Reference: 1181113

Published by Packt Publishing Ltd.
Livery Place
35 Livery Street
Birmingham B3 2PB, UK.

ISBN 978-1-78328-171-8

www.packtpub.com

Cover Image by Prashant Timappa Shetty (sparkling.spectrum.123@gmail.com)

Credits

Author
Danil Zburivsky

Reviewers
Skanda Bhargav
Yanick Champoux
Cyril Ganchev
Alan Gardner

Acquisition Editor
Joanne Fitzpatrick

Commissioning Editor
Amit Ghodake

Technical Editors
Venu Manthena
Pramod Kumavat

Project Coordinator
Amey Sawant

Copy Editors
Kirti Pai
Lavina Pereira
Adithi Shetty
Aditya Nair

Proofreader
Linda Morris

Indexer
Monica Ajmera Mehta

Graphics
Ronak Dhruv

Production Coordinator
Manu Joseph

Cover Work
Manu Joseph

About the Author

Danil Zburivsky is a database professional with a focus on open source technologies. Danil started his career as a MySQL database administrator and is currently working as a consultant at Pythian, a global data infrastructure management company. At Pythian, Danil was involved in building a number of Hadoop clusters for customers in financial, entertainment, and communication sectors.

Danil's other interests include writing fun things in Python, robotics, and machine learning. He is also a regular speaker at various industrial events.

I would like to thank my wife for agreeing to sacrifice most of our summer evenings while I was working on the book. I would also like to thank my colleagues from Pythian, especially Alan Gardner, Cyril Ganchev, and Yanick Champoux, who contributed a lot to this project.

About the Reviewers

Skanda Bhargav is an Engineering graduate from Visvesvaraya Technological University, Belgaum, Karnataka, India. He did his majors in Computer Science and Engineering. He is currently employed with an MNC based out of Bangalore. Skanda is a Cloudera Certified developer in Apache Hadoop. His interests are Big Data and Hadoop.

I would like to thank my family for their immense support and faith in me throughout my learning stage. My friends have brought my confidence to a level that brings out the best in me. I am happy that God has blessed me with such wonderful people around me, without which this work might not have been as successful as it is today

Yanick Champoux is currently sailing the Big Data seas as a solutions architect. In his spare time, he hacks Perl, grows orchids, and writes comic books.

Cyril Ganchev is a system administrator, database administrator, and a software developer living in Sofia, Bulgaria. He received a master's degree in Computer Systems and Technologies from the Technical University of Sofia in 2005.

In 2002, he started working as a system administrator in an Internet Café while studying at the Technical University of Sofia. In 2004, he began working as a software developer for the biggest Bulgarian IT company, Information Services Plc. He has been involved in many projects for the Bulgarian government, the Bulgarian National Bank, the National Revenue Agency, and others. He has been involved in several government elections in Bulgaria, writing the code that calculates the results.

Since 2012, he is working remotely for a Canadian company, Pythian. He started as an Oracle Database Administrator. In 2013, he transitioned to a newly formed team focused on Big Data and NoSQL.

Cyril Ganchev is an Oracle Advanced PL/SQL Developer Certified Professional and Oracle Database 11g Administrator Certified Associate.

I want to thank my parents for always supporting me, in all of my endeavors.

Alan Gardner is a solutions architect and developer specializing in designing Big Data systems. These systems incorporate technologies including Hadoop, Apache Kafka, and Storm, as well as Data Science techniques. Alan enjoys presenting his projects and shares his experience extensively at user groups and conferences. He also plays with functional programming and mobile and web development in his spare time.

Alan is also deeply involved in Ottawa's developer community, consulting with multiple organizations to help non-technical stakeholders organize developer events. With his group, Ottawa Drones, he runs hack days where developers can network, exchange ideas, and build their skills while programming flying robots.

I'd like to thank Paul White, Alex Gorbachev, and Mick Saunders for always helping me keep on the right path throughout different phases of my career, and Jasmin for always supporting me.

www.PacktPub.com

Support files, eBooks, discount offers and more

You might want to visit www.PacktPub.com for support files and downloads related to your book.

Did you know that Packt offers eBook versions of every book published, with PDF and ePub files available? You can upgrade to the eBook version at www.PacktPub.com and as a print book customer, you are entitled to a discount on the eBook copy. Get in touch with us at service@packtpub.com for more details.

At www.PacktPub.com, you can also read a collection of free technical articles, sign up for a range of free newsletters and receive exclusive discounts and offers on Packt books and eBooks.

http://PacktLib.PacktPub.com

Do you need instant solutions to your IT questions? PacktLib is Packt's online digital book library. Here, you can access, read and search across Packt's entire library of books.

Why Subscribe?

- Fully searchable across every book published by Packt
- Copy and paste, print and bookmark content
- On demand and accessible via web browser

Free Access for Packt account holders

If you have an account with Packt at www.PacktPub.com, you can use this to access PacktLib today and view nine entirely free books. Simply use your login credentials for immediate access.

Table of Contents

Preface

In the last couple of years, Hadoop has become a standard solution for building data integration platforms. Introducing any new technology into a company's data infrastructure stack requires system engineers and database administrators to quickly learn all the aspects of the new component. Hadoop doesn't make this task any easier because it is not a single software product, but it is rather a collection of multiple separate open source projects. These projects need to be properly installed and configured in order to make the Hadoop platform robust and reliable.

Many existing Hadoop distributions provide a simplified way to install Hadoop using some kind of graphical interface. This approach dramatically reduces the amount of time required to go from zero to the fully functional Hadoop cluster. It also simplifies managing the cluster configuration. The problem with an automated setup and configuration is that it actually hides a lot of important aspects about Hadoop components that work together, such as why some components require other components, and which configuration parameters are the most important, and so on.

This book provides a guide to installing and configuring all the main Hadoop components manually. Setting up at least one fully operational cluster by yourself will provide very useful insights into how Hadoop operates under the hood and will make it much easier for you to debug any issues that may arise. You can also use this book as a quick reference to the main Hadoop components and configuration options gathered in one place and in a succinct format. While writing this book, I found myself constantly referring to it when working on real production Hadoop clusters, to look up a specific variable or refresh a best practice when it comes to OS configuration. This habit reassured me that such a guide might be useful to other aspiring and experienced Hadoop administrators and developers.

What this book covers

Chapter 1, Setting Up Hadoop Cluster – from Hardware to Distribution, reviews the main Hadoop components and approaches for choosing and sizing cluster hardware. It also touches on the topic of various Hadoop distributions.

Chapter 2, Installing and Configuring Hadoop, provides step-by-step instructions for installing and configuring the main Hadoop components: NameNode (including High Availability), JobTracker, DataNodes, and TaskTrackers.

Chapter 3, Configuring the Hadoop Ecosystem, reviews configuration procedures for Sqoop, Hive, and Impala.

Chapter 4, Securing Hadoop Installation, provides guidelines to securing various Hadoop components. It also provides an overview of configuring Kerberos with Hadoop.

Chapter 5, Monitoring Hadoop Cluster, guides you to getting your cluster ready for production usage.

Chapter 6, Deploying Hadoop to the Cloud, reviews using Hadoop in virtualized environments, including Elastic MapReduce and using Whirr.

What you need for this book

There are no specific software requirements for the examples in this book. If you plan to install a Hadoop cluster in a sandbox environment, you will need some kind of virtualization software such as Virtual Box.

Who this book is for

This book is mainly for people who plan to install, configure, and support production -Hadoop clusters. This could be a system administrator, database administrators, or Hadoop administrators (still a rare job title these days). In general, it would be interesting for anyone who plans to work with the Hadoop platform.

Conventions

In this book, you will find a number of styles of text that distinguish between different kinds of information. Here are some examples of these styles, and an explanation of their meaning.

Code words in text, database table names, folder names, filenames, file extensions, pathnames, dummy URLs, user input, and Twitter handles are shown as follows: "You need to specify the connection string for all those Metastores in the `hive.metastore.uris` variable."

A block of code is set as follows:

```
{
"access_id": "Your Access Key ID",
"private_key": "Your AWS Secret Access Key",
"keypair": "emr-keys",
"key-pair-file": "/path/to/key-file/emr-keys.pem",
"log_uri": "s3n://emr-logs-x123/",
"egion": "us-east-1"
}
```

When we wish to draw your attention to a particular part of a code block, the relevant lines or items are set in bold:

```
{
"access_id": "Your Access Key ID",
"private_key": "Your AWS Secret Access Key",
"keypair": "emr-keys",
"key-pair-file": "/path/to/key-file/emr-keys.pem",
"log_uri": "s3n://emr-logs-x123/",
"egion": "us-east-1"
}
```

Any command-line input or output is written as follows:

```
# hdfs dfs -mkdir /warehouse
# hdfs dfs -chmod a+w /warehouse
```

New terms and **important words** are shown in bold. Words that you see on the screen, in menus or dialog boxes for example, appear in the text like this: "clicking the **Next** button moves you to the next screen".

 Warnings or important notes appear in a box like this.

 Tips and tricks appear like this.

Reader feedback

Feedback from our readers is always welcome. Let us know what you think about this book—what you liked or may have disliked. Reader feedback is important for us to develop titles that you really get the most out of.

To send us general feedback, simply send an e-mail to feedback@packtpub.com, and mention the book title via the subject of your message.

If there is a topic that you have expertise in and you are interested in either writing or contributing to a book, see our author guide on www.packtpub.com/authors.

Customer support

Now that you are the proud owner of a Packt book, we have a number of things to help you to get the most from your purchase.

Errata

Although we have taken every care to ensure the accuracy of our content, mistakes do happen. If you find a mistake in one of our books—maybe a mistake in the text or the code—we would be grateful if you would report this to us. By doing so, you can save other readers from frustration and help us improve subsequent versions of this book. If you find any errata, please report them by visiting http://www.packtpub.com/submit-errata, selecting your book, clicking on the **errata submission form** link, and entering the details of your errata. Once your errata are verified, your submission will be accepted and the errata will be uploaded on our website, or added to any list of existing errata, under the Errata section of that title. Any existing errata can be viewed by selecting your title from http://www.packtpub.com/support.

Piracy

Piracy of copyright material on the Internet is an ongoing problem across all media. At Packt, we take the protection of our copyright and licenses very seriously. If you come across any illegal copies of our works, in any form, on the Internet, please provide us with the location address or website name immediately so that we can pursue a remedy.

Please contact us at copyright@packtpub.com with a link to the suspected pirated material.

We appreciate your help in protecting our authors, and our ability to bring you valuable content.

Questions

You can contact us at questions@packtpub.com if you are having a problem with any aspect of the book, and we will do our best to address it.

1
Setting Up Hadoop Cluster – from Hardware to Distribution

Hadoop is a free and open source distributed storage and computational platform. It was created to allow storing and processing large amounts of data using clusters of commodity hardware. In the last couple of years, Hadoop became a de facto standard for the big data projects. In this chapter, we will cover the following topics:

- Choosing Hadoop cluster hardware
- Hadoop distributions
- Choosing OS for the Hadoop cluster

This chapter will give an overview of the Hadoop philosophy when it comes to choosing and configuring hardware for the cluster. We will also review the different Hadoop distributions, the number of which is growing every year. This chapter will explain the similarities and differences between those distributions.

For you, as a Hadoop administrator or an architect, the practical part of cluster implementation starts with making decisions on what kind of hardware to use and how much of it you will need, but there are some essential questions that need to be asked before you can place your hardware order, roll up your sleeves, and start setting things up. Among such questions are those related to cluster design, such as how much data will the cluster need to store, what are the projections of data growth rate, what would be the main data access pattern, will the cluster be used mostly for predefined scheduled tasks, or will it be a multitenant environment used for exploratory data analysis? Hadoop's architecture and data access model allows great flexibility. It can accommodate different types of workload, such as batch processing huge amounts of data or supporting real-time analytics with projects like Impala.

At the same time, some clusters are better suited for specific types of work and hence it is important to arrive at the hardware specification phase with the ideas about cluster design and purpose in mind. When dealing with clusters of hundreds of servers, initial decisions about hardware and general layout will have a significant influence on a cluster's performance, stability, and associated costs.

Choosing Hadoop cluster hardware

Hadoop is a scalable clustered non-shared system for massively parallel data processing. The whole concept of Hadoop is that a single node doesn't play a significant role in the overall cluster reliability and performance. This design assumption leads to choosing hardware that can efficiently process small (relative to total data size) amounts of data on a single node and doesn't require lots of reliability and redundancy on a hardware level. As you may already know, there are several types of servers that comprise the Hadoop cluster. There are master nodes, such as **NameNode**, **Secondary NameNode**, and **JobTracker** and worker nodes that are called **DataNodes**. In addition to the core Hadoop components, it is a common practice to deploy several auxiliary servers, such as Gateways, Hue server, and Hive Metastore. A typical Hadoop cluster can look like the following diagram:

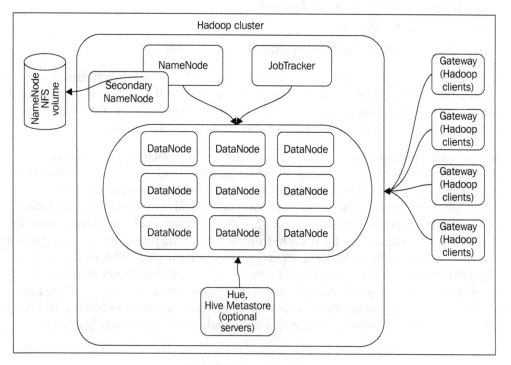

Typical Hadoop cluster layout

The roles that those types of servers play in a cluster are different, so are the requirements for hardware specifications and reliability of these nodes. We will first discuss different hardware configurations for DataNodes and then will talk about typical setups for NameNode and JobTracker.

Choosing the DataNode hardware

DataNode is the main worker node in a Hadoop cluster and it plays two main roles: it stores pieces of HDFS data and executes **MapReduce** tasks. DataNode is Hadoop's primary storage and computational resource. One may think that since DataNodes play such an important role in a cluster, you should use the best hardware available for them. This is not entirely true. Hadoop was designed with an idea that DataNodes are "disposable workers", servers that are fast enough to do useful work as a part of the cluster, but cheap enough to be easily replaced if they fail. Frequency of hardware failures in large clusters is probably one of the most important considerations that core Hadoop developers had in mind. Hadoop addresses this issue by moving the redundancy implementation from the cluster hardware to the cluster software itself.

Hadoop provides redundancy on many levels. Each DataNode stores only some blocks for the HDFS files and those blocks are replicated multiple times to different nodes, so in the event of a single server failure, data remains accessible. The cluster can even tolerate multiple nodes' failure, depending on the configuration you choose. Hadoop goes beyond that and allows you to specify which servers reside on which racks and tries to store copies of data on separate racks, thus, significantly increasing probability that your data remains accessible even if the whole rack goes down (though this is not a strict guarantee). This design means that there is no reason to invest into the RAID controller for Hadoop DataNodes.

Instead of using RAID for local disks, a setup that is known as JBOD (Just a Bunch of Disks) is a preferred choice. It provides better performance for Hadoop workload and reduces hardware costs. You don't have to worry about individual disk failure since redundancy is provided by HDFS.

Storing data is the first role that DataNode plays. The second role is to serve as a data processing node and execute custom MapReduce code. MapReduce jobs are split into lots of separate tasks, which are executed in parallel on multiple DataNodes and for a job to produce logically consistent results, all subtasks must be completed.

This means that Hadoop has to provide redundancy not only on storage, but also on a computational layer. Hadoop achieves this by retrying failed tasks on different nodes, without interrupting the whole job. It also keeps track of nodes that have abnormally high rate of failures or have been responding slower than others and eventually such nodes can be blacklisted and excluded from the cluster.

So, what should the hardware for a typical DataNode look like? Ideally, DataNode should be a balanced system with a reasonable amount of disk storage and processing power. Defining "balanced system" and "reasonable amount of storage" is not as simple a task as it may sound. There are many factors that come into play when you are trying to spec out an optimal and scalable Hadoop cluster. One of the most important considerations is total cluster storage capacity and cluster storage density. These parameters are tightly related. Total cluster storage capacity is relatively simple to estimate. It basically answers questions such as how much data we can put into the cluster. The following is a list of steps that you can take to estimate the required capacity for your cluster:

1. **Identify data sources**: List out all known data sources and decide whether full or partial initial data import will be required. You should reserve 15-20 percent of your total cluster capacity, or even more to accommodate any new data sources or unplanned data size growth.

2. **Estimate data growth rate**: Each identified data source will have a data ingestion rate associated with it. For example, if you are planning to do daily exports from your OLTP database, you can easily estimate how much data this source will produce over the course of the week, month, year, and so on. You will need to do some test exports to get an accurate number.

3. **Multiply your estimated storage requirements by a replication factor**: So far, we talked about the usable storage capacity. Hadoop achieves redundancy on the HDFS level by copying data blocks several times and placing them on different nodes in the cluster. By default, each block is replicated three times. You can adjust this parameter, both by increasing or decreasing the replication factor. Setting the replication factor to 1 completely diminishes a cluster's reliability and should not be used. So, to get raw cluster storage capacity, you need to multiply your estimates by a replication factor. If you estimated that you need 300 TB of usable storage this year and you are planning to use a replication factor of 3, your raw capacity will be 900 TB.

4. **Factoring in MapReduce temporary files and system data**: MapReduce tasks produce intermediate data that is being passed from the map execution phase to the reduce phase. This temporary data doesn't reside on HDFS, but you need to allocate about 25-30 percent of total server disk capacity for temporary files. Additionally, you will need separate disk volumes for an operating system, but storage requirements for OS are usually insignificant.

Identifying total usable and raw cluster storage capacity is the first step in nailing down hardware specifications for the DataNode. For further discussions, we will mean raw capacity when referring to cluster's total available storage, since this is what's important from the hardware perspective. Another important metric is storage density, which is the total cluster storage capacity divided by the number of DataNodes in the cluster. Generally, you have two choices: either deploy lots of servers with low storage density, or use less servers with higher storage density. We will review both the options and outline the pros and cons for each.

Low storage density cluster

Historically, Hadoop clusters were deployed on reasonably low storage density servers. This allowed scaling clusters to petabytes of storage capacity using low capacity hard drives available on the market at that time. While the hard drive capacity increased significantly over the last several years, using a large low-density cluster is still a valid option for many. Cost is the main reason you will want to go this route. Individual Hadoop node performance is driven not only by storage capacity, but rather by a balance that you have between RAM/CPU and disks. Having lots of storage on every DataNode, but not having enough RAM and CPU resources to process all the data, will not be beneficial in most cases.

It is always hard to give specific recommendations about the Hadoop cluster hardware. A balanced setup will depend on the cluster workload, as well as the allocated budget. New hardware appears on the market all the time, so any considerations should be adjusted accordingly. To illustrate hardware selection logic for a low density cluster, we will use the following example:

Let's assume we have picked up a server with 6 HDD slots. If we choose reasonably priced 2 TB hard drives, it will give us 12 TB of raw capacity per server.

 There is little reason to choose faster 15000 rpm drives for your cluster. Sequential read/write performance matters much more for Hadoop cluster, than random access speed. 7200 rpm drives are a preferred choice in most cases.

For a low density server, our main aim is to keep the cost low to be able to afford a large number of machines. 2 x 4 core CPUs match this requirement and will give reasonable processing power. Each map or reduce task will utilize a single CPU core, but since some time will be spent waiting on IO, it is OK to oversubscribe the CPU core. With 8 cores available, we can configure about 12 map/reduce slots per node.

Each task will require from 2 to 4 GB of RAM. 36 GB of RAM is a reasonable choice for this type of server, but going with 48 GB is ideal. Note that we are trying to balance different components. It's of little use to significantly increase the amount of RAM for this configuration, because you will not be able to schedule enough tasks on one node to properly utilize it.

Let's say you are planning to store 500 TB of data in your cluster. With the default replication factor of 3, this will result in 1500 TB of raw capacity. If you use low density DataNode configuration, you will need 63 servers to satisfy this requirement. If you double the required capacity, you will need more than 100 servers in your cluster. Managing a large number of servers has lots of challenges of its own. You will need to think if there is enough physical room in your data center to host additional racks. Additional power consumption and air conditioning also present significant challenges when the number of servers grows. To address these problems, you can increase the storage capacity of an individual server, as well as tune up other hardware specs.

High storage density cluster

Many companies are looking into building smaller Hadoop clusters, but with more storage and computational power per server. Besides addressing issues mentioned above, such clusters can be a better fit for workload where huge amounts of storage are not a priority. Such workload is computationally intensive and includes machine learning, exploratory analytics, and other problems.

The logic behind choosing and balancing hardware components for a high density cluster is the same as for a lower density one. As an example of such a configuration, we will choose a server with 16 x 2 TB hard drives or 24 x 1 TB hard drives. Having more lower capacity disks per server is preferable, because it will provide better IO throughput and better fault tolerance. To increase the computational power of the individual machine, we will use 16 CPU cores and 96 GB of RAM.

NameNode and JobTracker hardware configuration

Hadoop implements a centralized coordination model, where there is a node (or a group of nodes) whose role is to coordinate tasks among servers that comprise the cluster. The server that is responsible for HDFS coordination is called NameNode and the server responsible for MapReduce jobs dispatching is called JobTracker. Actually NameNode and JobTracker are just separate Hadoop processes, but due to their critical role in almost all cases, these services run on dedicated machines.

The NameNode hardware

NameNode is critical to HDFS availability. It stores all the filesystem metadata: which blocks comprise which files, on which DataNodes these blocks can be found, how many free blocks are available, and which servers can host them. Without NameNode, data in HDFS is almost completely useless. The data is actually still there, but without NameNode you will not be able to reconstruct files from data blocks, nor will you be able to upload new data. For a long time, NameNode was a single point of failure, which was less than ideal for a system that advertises high fault tolerance and redundancy of most components and processes. This was addressed with the introduction of the NameNode High Availability setup in Apache Hadoop 2.0.0, but still hardware requirements for NameNode are very different from what was outlined for DataNode in the previous section. Let's start with the memory estimates for NameNode. NameNode has to store all HDFS metadata info, including files, directories' structures, and blocks allocation in memory. This may sound like a wasteful usage of RAM, but NameNode has to guarantee fast access to files on hundreds or thousands of machines, so using hard drives for accessing this information would be too slow. According to the Apache Hadoop documentation, each HDFS block will occupy approximately 250 bytes of RAM on NameNode, plus an additional 250 bytes will be required for each file and directory. Let's say you have 5,000 files with an average of 20 GB per file. If you use the default HDFS block file size of 64 MB and a replication factor of 3, your NameNode will need to hold information about 50 million blocks, which will require 50 million x 250 bytes plus filesystem overhead equals 1.5 GB of RAM. This is not as much as you may have imagined, but in most cases a Hadoop cluster has many more files in total and since each file will consist of at least one block, memory usage on NameNode will be much higher. There is no penalty for having more RAM on the NameNode than your cluster requires at the moment, so overprovisioning is fine. Systems with 64-96 GB of RAM are a good choice for the NameNode server.

To guarantee persistency of filesystem metadata, NameNode has to keep a copy of its memory structures on disk as well. For this, NameNode maintains a file called editlog, which captures all changes that are happening to the HDFS, such as new files and directories creation and replication factor changes. This is very similar to the redo logfiles that most relational databases use. In addition to editlog, NameNode maintains a full snapshot of the current HDFS metadata state in an fsimage file. In case of a restart, or server crash, NameNode will use the latest fsimage and apply all the changes from the editlog file that needs to be applied to restore a valid point-in-time state of the filesystem.

Unlike traditional database systems, NameNode delegates the task of periodically applying changes from editlog to fsimage to a separate server called Secondary NameNode. This is done to keep the editlog file size under control, because changes that are already applied to fsimage are no longer required in the logfile and also to minimize the recovery time. Since these files are mirroring data structures that NameNode keeps in memory, disk space requirements for them are normally pretty low. fsimage will not grow bigger than the amount of RAM you allocated for NameNode and editlog will be rotated once it has reached 64 MB by default. This means that you can keep the disk space requirements for NameNode in the 500 GB range. Using RAID on the NameNode makes a lot of sense, because it provides protection of critical data from individual disk crashes. Besides serving filesystem requests from HDFS clients, NameNode also has to process heartbeat messages from all DataNodes in the cluster. This type of workload requires significant CPU resources, so it's a good idea to provision 8-16 CPU cores for NameNode, depending on the planned cluster size.

In this book, we will focus on setting up NameNode HA, which will require Primary and Standby NameNodes to be identical in terms of hardware. More details on how to achieve high availability for NameNode will be provided in *Chapter 2, Installing and Configuring Hadoop*.

The JobTracker hardware

Besides NameNode and Secondary NameNode, there is another master server in the Hadoop cluster called the **JobTracker**. Conceptually, it plays a similar role for the MapReduce framework as NameNode does for HDFS. JobTracker is responsible for submitting user jobs to TaskTrackers, which are services running on each DataNode. TaskTrackers send periodic heartbeat messages to JobTracker, reporting current status of running jobs, available map/reduce slots, and so on. Additionally, JobTracker keeps a history of the last executed jobs (number is configurable) in memory and provides access to Hadoop-specific or user-defined counters associated with the jobs. While RAM availability is critical to JobTracker, its memory footprint is normally smaller than that of NameNode. Having 24-48 GB of RAM for mid- and large-size clusters is a reasonable estimate. You can review this number if your cluster will be a multitenant environment with thousands of users. By default, JobTracker doesn't save any state information to the disk and uses persistent storage only for logging purpose. This means that total disk requirements for this service are minimal. Just like NameNode, JobTracker will need to be able to process huge amounts of heartbeat information from TaskTrackers, accept and dispatch incoming user jobs, and also apply job scheduling algorithms to be able to utilize a cluster most efficiently. These are highly CPU-intensive tasks, so make sure you invest in fast multi-core processors, similar to what you would pick up for NameNode.

All three types of master nodes are critical to Hadoop cluster availability. If you lose a NameNode server, you will lose access to HDFS data. Issues with Secondary NameNode will not cause an immediate outage, but will delay the filesystem checkpointing process. Similarly, a crash of JobTracker will cause all running MapReduce jobs to abort and no new jobs will be able to run. All these consequences require a different approach to the master's hardware selection than what we have discussed for DataNode. Using RAID arrays for critical data volumes, redundant network and power supplies, and potentially higher-grade enterprise level hardware components is a preferred choice.

Gateway and other auxiliary services

Gateway servers are a client's access points to the Hadoop cluster. Interaction with data in HDFS requires having connectivity between the client program and all nodes inside the cluster. This is not always practical from a network design and security perspective. Gateways are usually deployed outside of the primary cluster subnet and are used for data imports and other user programs. Additional infrastructure components and different shells can be deployed on standalone servers, or combined with other services. Hardware requirements to these optional services are obviously much lower than those for cluster nodes and often you can deploy gateways on virtual machines. 4-8 CPU cores and 16-24 GB of RAM is a reasonable configuration for a Gateway node.

Network considerations

In Hadoop cluster, network is a component that is as important as a CPU, disk, or RAM. HDFS relies on network communication to update NameNode on a current filesystem status, as well as to receive and send data blocks to the client. MapReduce jobs also use the network for status messages, but additionally uses bandwidth when a file block has to be read from a DataNode that is not local to the current TaskTracker, and to send intermediate data from mappers to the reducers. In short, there is a lot of network activity going on in a Hadoop cluster. As of now, there are two main choices when it comes to the network hardware. A 1 GbE network is cheap, but is rather limited in throughput, while a 10 GbE network can significantly increase the costs of a large Hadoop deployment. Like every other component of the cluster, the network choice will depend on the intended cluster layout.

For larger clusters, we came up with generally lower spec machines, with less disks, RAM, and CPU per node, assuming that a large volume of such servers will provide enough capacity. For the smaller cluster, we have chosen high-end servers. We can use the same arguments when it comes to choosing which network architecture to apply.

For clusters with multiple less powerful nodes, installing 10 GbE makes little sense for two reasons. First of all, it will increase the total cost of building the cluster significantly and you may not be able to utilize all the available network capacity. For example, with six disks per DataNode, you should be able to achieve about 420 MB/sec of local write throughput, which is less than the network bandwidth. This means that the cluster bottleneck will shift from the network to the disks' IO capacity. On the other hand, a smaller cluster of fast servers with lots of storage will most probably choke on a 1 GbE network and most of the server's available resources will be wasted. Since such clusters are normally smaller, a 10 GbE network hardware will not have as big of an impact on the budget as for a larger setup.

 Most of the modern servers come with several network controllers. You can use bonding to increase network throughput.

Hadoop hardware summary

Let's summarize the possible Hadoop hardware configurations required for different types of clusters.

DataNode for low storage density cluster:

Component	Specification
Storage	6-8 2 TB hard drives per server, JBOD setup, no RAID
CPU	8 CPU cores
RAM	32-48 GB per node
Network	1 GbE interfaces, bonding of several NICs for higher throughput is possible

DataNode for high storage density cluster

Component	Specification
Storage	16-24 1 TB hard drives per server, JBOD setup, no RAID
CPU	16 CPU cores
RAM	64-96 GB per node
Network	10 GbE network interface

NameNode and Standby NameNode

Component	Specification
Storage	Low disk space requirements: 500 GB should be enough in most cases. RAID 10 or RAID 5 for `fsimage` and `editlog`. Network attached storage to place a copy of these files
CPU	8-16 CPU cores, depending on the cluster size
RAM	64-96 GB
Network	1 GbE or 10 GbE interfaces, bonding of several NICs for higher throughput is possible

JobTracker

Component	Specification
Storage	Low disk space requirements: 500 GB should be enough in most cases for logfiles and the job's state information
CPU	8-16 CPU cores, depending on the cluster size
RAM	64-96 GB.
Network	1 GbE or 10 GbE interfaces, bonding of several NICs for higher throughput is possible

Hadoop distributions

Hadoop comes in many different flavors. There are many different versions and many different distributions available from a number of companies. There are several key players in this area today and we will discuss what options they provide.

Hadoop versions

Hadoop releasing a versioning system is, to say the least, confusing. There are several branches with different stable versions available and it is important to understand what features each branch provides (or excludes). As of now, these are the following Hadoop versions available: 0.23, 1.0, and 2.0. Surprisingly, higher versions do not always include all the features from the lower versions. For example, 0.23 includes NameNode High Availability and NameNode Federation, but drops support for the traditional MaprReduce framework (MRv1) in favor of a new YARN framework (MRv2).

MRv2 is compatible with MRv1 on the API level, but a daemon's setup and configuration, and concepts are different. Version 1.0 still includes MRv1, but lacks NameNode HA and Federation features, which many consider critical for production usage. Version 2.0 is actually based on 0.23 and has the same feature set, but will be used for future development and releases. One of the reasons that Hadoop released versions seem not to follow straightforward logic, is that Hadoop is still a relatively new technology and many features that are highly desirable by some users can introduce instability and sometimes they require significant code changes and approach changes, such as in a case with YARN. This leads to lots of different code branches with different stable release versions and lots of confusion to the end user. Since the purpose of this book is to guide you through planning and implementing the production Hadoop cluster, we will focus on stable Hadoop versions that provide proven solutions such as MRv1, but will also include important availability features for the NameNode. As you can see, this will narrow down the choice of a Hadoop release version right away.

Choosing Hadoop distribution

Apache Hadoop is not the only distribution available. There are several other companies that maintain their own forks of the project, both free and proprietary. You probably have already started seeing why this would make sense: streamlining the release process for Hadoop and combining different features from several Hadoop branches makes it much easier for the end user to implement a cluster. One of the most popular non-Apache distributions of Hadoop is **Cloudera Hadoop Distribution** or **CDH**.

Cloudera Hadoop distribution

Cloudera is the company that provides commercial support, professional services, and advanced tools for Hadoop. Their CDH distribution is free and open source under the same Apache 2.0 license. What makes CDH appealing to the end user is that there are fewer code branches, version numbers are aligned, and critical bug fixes are backported to older versions. At this time, the latest major CDH release version is CDH4, which combines features from Apache 2.0 and 1.0 releases. It includes NameNode HA and Federation, supports both MRv1 and MRv2, which none of the Apache releases does at the moment. Another valuable feature that CDH provides, is integration of different Hadoop ecosystem projects. HDFS and MapReduce are core components of Hadoop, but over time many new projects were built on top of these components. These projects make Hadoop more user-friendly, speed up development cycles, build multitier MapReduce jobs easily, and so on.

One of the projects available in CDH that is gaining a lot of attention is Impala, which allows running real-time queries on Hadoop, bypassing MapReduce layer completely and accessing data directly from HDFS. Having dozens of ecosystem components, each with its own compatibility requirements and a variety of Apache Hadoop branches, does not make integration an easy task. CDH solves this problem for you by providing core Hadoop and most of the popular ecosystem projects that are compatible and tested with each other in one distribution. This is a big advantage for the user and it made CDH the most popular Hadoop distribution at the moment (according to Google Trends). In addition to CDH, Cloudera also distributes Cloudera Manager—a web based management tool to provision, configure, and monitor your Hadoop cluster. Cloudera Manager comes in both free and paid enterprise versions.

Hortonworks Hadoop distribution

Another popular Hadoop distribution is Hortonworks Data Platform (HDP), by Hortonworks. Similarly to Cloudera, Hortonworks provides a pre-packaged distribution of core and ecosystem Hadoop projects, as well as commercial support and services for it. As of now, the latest stable version of HDP 1.2 and 2.0 is in Alpha stage; both are based on Apache Hadoop 1.0 and 2.0 accordingly. HDP 1.2 provides several features that are not included in the CDH or Apache distribution. Hortonworks implemented NameNode HA on Hadoop 1.0, not by back porting JournalNodes and Quorum-based storage from Apache Hadoop 2.0, but rather by implementing cold cluster failover based on Linux HA solutions. HDP also includes HCatalog—a service that provides an integration point for projects like Pig and Hive. Hortonworks makes a bet on integrating Hadoop with traditional BI tools, an area that has lots of interest from existing and potential Hadoop users. HDP includes an ODBC driver for Hive, which is claimed to be compatible with most existing BI tools. Another unique HDP feature is its availability on the Windows platform. Bringing Hadoop to the Windows world will have a big impact on the platform's adoption rates and can make HDP a leading distribution for this operating system, but unfortunately this is still in alpha version and can't be recommended for the production usage at the moment. When it comes to cluster management and monitoring, HDP includes Apache Ambari, which is a web-based tool, similar to Cloudera Manager, but is 100 percent free and open source with no distinction between free and enterprise versions.

MapR

While Cloudera and Hortonworks provide the most popular Hadoop distributions, they are not the only companies that use Hadoop as a foundation for their products. There are several projects that should be mentioned here. MapR is a company that provides a Hadoop-based platform. There are several different versions of their product: M3 is a free version with limited features, and M5 and M7 are Enterprise level commercial editions. MapR takes a different approach than Cloudera or Hortonworks. Their software is not free, but has some features that can be appealing to the Enterprise users. The major difference of the MapR platform from Apache Hadoop is that instead of HDFS, a different proprietary filesystem called MapR-FS is used. MapR-FS is implemented in C++ and provides lower latency and higher concurrency access than Java-based HDFS. It is compatible with Hadoop on an API level, but it's a completely different implementation. Other MapR-FS features include the ability to mount Hadoop cluster as an NFS volume, cluster-wide snapshots, and cluster mirroring. Obviously, all these features rely on the MapR-FS implementation.

As you can see, the modern Hadoop landscape is far from being plain. There are many options to choose from. It is easy to narrow down the list of available options when you consider requirements for production cluster. Production Hadoop version needs to be stable and well tested. It needs to include important components, such as NameNode HA and proved MRv1 framework. For you, as a Hadoop administrator, it is important to be able to easily install Hadoop on multiple nodes, without a need to handpick required components and worry about compatibility. These requirements will quickly draw your attention to distributions like CDH or HDP. The rest of this book will be focused around CDH distribution as it is the most popular choice for production installations right now. CDH also provides a rich features set and good stability. It is worth mentioning that Hadoop 2 got its first GA release while this book was in progress. Hadoop 2 brings in many new features such as NameNode High Availability, which were previously available only in CDH.

Choosing OS for the Hadoop cluster

Choosing an operating system for your future Hadoop cluster is a relatively simple task. Hadoop core and its ecosystem components are all written in Java, with a few exceptions. While Java code itself is cross-platform, currently Hadoop only runs on Linux-like systems. The reason for this is that too many design decisions were made with Linux in mind, which made the code surrounding core Hadoop components such as `start/stop` scripts and permissions model dependent on the Linux environment.

When it comes to Linux, Hadoop is pretty indifferent to specific implementations and runs well on different varieties of this OS: Red Hat, CentOS, Debian, Ubuntu, Suse, and Fedora. All these distributions don't have specific requirements for running Hadoop. In general, nothing prevents Hadoop from successfully working on any other POSIX-style OS, such as Solaris or BSD, if you make sure that all dependencies are resolved properly and all shell supporting scripts are working. Still, most of the production installations of Hadoop are running on Linux and this is the OS that we will be focusing on in our further discussions. Specifically, examples in this book will be focused on CentOS, since it is one of the popular choices for the production system, as well as its twin, Red Hat.

Apache Hadoop provides source binaries, as well as **RPM** and **DEB** packages for stable releases. Currently, this is a 1.0 branch. Building Hadoop from the source code, while still being an option, is not recommended for most of the users, since it requires experience in assembling big Java-based projects and careful dependencies resolution. Both Cloudera and Hortonworks distributions provide an easy way to setup a repository on your servers and install all required packages from there.

 There is no strict requirement to run the same operating system across all Hadoop nodes, but common sense suggests, that the lesser the deviation in nodes configuration, the easier it is to administer and manage it.

Summary

Building a production Hadoop cluster is a complex task with many steps involved. One of the often-overlooked steps in planning the cluster is outlining what kind of workload the future cluster will handle. As you have seen in this chapter, understanding what type of cluster you are building is important for proper sizing and choosing the right hardware configuration. Hadoop was originally designed for commodity hardware, but now it is being adopted by companies whose use cases are different from web giants like Yahoo! and Facebook. Such companies have different goals and resources and should plan their Hadoop cluster accordingly. It is not uncommon to see smaller clusters with more powerful nodes being built to save real estate in the data centers, as well as to keep power consumption under control.

Hadoop is constantly evolving with new features being added all the time and new important ecosystem projects emerging. Very often, these changes affect the core Hadoop components and new versions may not always be compatible with the old ones. There are several distributions of Hadoop that an end user can choose from, all providing a good level of integration between the components and even some additional features. It is often tempting to choose the latest and the most feature-rich version of Hadoop, but from a reliability perspective, it's better to go with the version that saw some production burn-in time and is stable enough. This will save you from unpleasant surprises. In the next chapter, we will dive into details about installing and configuring core Hadoop components. Roll up your sleeves and get ready to get your hands dirty!

2
Installing and Configuring Hadoop

After you have decided on your cluster layout and size, it is time to get Hadoop installed and get the cluster operational. We will walk you through the installation and configuration steps for three core Hadoop components: NameNode, DataNode, and JobTracker. We will also review different options for configuring NameNode High Availability and ways of quickly assessing cluster's health and performance. By the end of this chapter, you should have your Hadoop cluster up and running. We will keep the structure of the cluster similar to what was outlined in *Chapter 1, Setting Up Hadoop Cluster – from Hardware to Distribution*.

Configuring OS for Hadoop cluster

As mentioned earlier, Hadoop can run on almost any modern flavor of Linux. Instructions in this, and following chapters, will be focused on CentOS 6.x – CentOS and Red Hat are the most popular choices for production related Hadoop installations. It shouldn't be too hard to adopt these instructions for, let's say Debian, because all things that are directly related to configuring Hadoop components will stay the same and you should be able to substitute package managers for your favorite distributions easily.

Choosing and setting up the filesystem

Modern Linux distributions support different filesystems: EXT3, EXT4, XFS, BTRFS, among others. These filesystems possess slightly different characteristics when it comes to its performance on certain workloads.

If you favor stability over performance and advanced features, you might want to use EXT3, which is battle-tested on some of the largest Hadoop clusters. The complete list can be seen at http://wiki.apache.org/hadoop/DiskSetup. We will use EXT4 for our cluster setup, since it provides better performance on large files, which makes it a good candidate for Hadoop.

To format a volume using EXT4 filesystem, run the following command as a root user in your shell:

```
# mkfs -t ext4 -m 0 -O extent,sparse_super,flex_bg /dev/sdb1
```

In this example, partition 1 on drive b will be formatted. There are several options in the format command that need to be explained.

- `-m 0`: This option reduces the space reserved for a super-user to 0 percent from the default value of 5 percent. This can save a significant amount of disk space on large filesystems. If you have 16 TB per server, you will save about 800 GB.

- `-O extent,sparse_super,flex_bg`: This option will enable extent-based allocation, which will increase performance on large sequential IO requests. The `sparse_super` option is another disk space saving option. You can save space on large filesystems by allocating less superblock backup copies. The `flex_bg` option forces the filesystem to pack metadata blocks closed together, providing some performance improvements.

There are a couple of important options you need to know when mounting the filesystem. Those are `noatime` and `noadirtime`. By default, a filesystem would keep track of all operations, including reading a file or accessing a directory, by updating a metadata timestamp field. This can cause a significant overhead on a busy system and should be disabled. Here is an example of how to disable this feature in /etc/fstab:

```
/dev/sda1 /disk1 ext4 noatime,noadirtime 1 2
/dev/sdb1 /disk2 ext4 noatime,noadirtime 1 2
```

> Keep in mind that these disk configuration options are applied only on DataNode data disks. It is recommended to have RAID configured for NameNode volumes. RAID configuration is specific to your controller manufacturer.

Setting up Java Development Kit

Since Hadoop is written in Java, you need to make sure that a proper version of JDK is installed on all Hadoop nodes. It is absolutely critical to make sure that the version and distribution of JDK is the same on all nodes. Currently, the only officially supported distribution of JVM is Oracle JVM. There are reports that Hadoop can be built and run fine on OpenJDK, but we will stick to Oracle JDK. At the time of writing this book, Hadoop was tested to work on Java Version 6, while the current Oracle Java version is 7, and Java 6 actually reached the end of its life in February 2013. You can see the list of all the Java versions Hadoop has been tested against at `http://wiki.apache.org/hadoop/HadoopJavaVersions`. CentOS doesn't include Oracle JDK in the repositories, so you will need to download and install it separately. Download archived rpms from `http://www.oracle.com/technetwork/java/javase/downloads/jdk6downloads-1902814.html` (or Google `Oracle Java 6 download` in case the link changes). It is OK to choose the latest 6.x version, since new updates and security patches are being released quite often. Make sure you go for an rpm install. We will use Cloudera's Distribution, including Apache Hadoop (**CDH**) packages to install Hadoop in further sections, which rely on Oracle Java rpms. Here is how you install the 64-bit Oracle Java Version 1.6.0_45:

```
# chmod 755 jdk-6u45-linux-x64-rpm.bin
# ./jdk-6u45-linux-x64-rpm.bin
```

Make sure you repeat this step on all Hadoop nodes, including Gateway servers.

Other OS settings

There are several other operating system settings that you need to change to ensure proper operation of the Hadoop cluster. First of all, you need to make sure that the hostname/IP resolution is working properly across the cluster. When Hadoop master nodes, such as NameNode or JobTracker, receive a heartbeat message from a new DataNode for the first time, they record its IP address and use it for further communications. So, it is important to configure proper hostnames for all nodes in the cluster, and to make sure they resolve to correct IP addresses using the `/etc/hosts` file. To make sure the host reports the correct IP address, use the `ping` command and check the IP address returned. Here is an example of what `/etc/hosts` may look like:

```
127.0.0.1    localhost.localdomain localhost
::1          localhost.localdomain localhost
192.168.0.100 nn1.hadoop.test.com nn1
192.168.0.101 sn1.hadoop.test.com sn1
```

```
192.168.0.102  jt1.hadoop.test.com jt1
192.168.0.40   dn1.hadoop.test.com dn1
192.168.0.41   dn2.hadoop.test.com dn2
```

 It's a good practice to give meaningful names to the nodes in the cluster, so the name reflects a function the host plays. Such an approach will make it easy to generate hosts/IP lists with a script and propagate it on all the servers.

Setting up the CDH repositories

There are many ways to install Hadoop, depending on which distribution you choose. Even within one distribution, you can choose different routes. CDH provides various assisted modes of installing Hadoop packages on your cluster: you can use the Cloudera Manager web interface to perform autodiscovery of the nodes in your cluster and install and preconfigure appropriate packages for you, or you can set up the CDH repository and install components manually. In this book, we will go with manual install, because it will help to better understand Hadoop mechanics and how different components interact with each other. We will still use a **yum** package management utility to take care of copying files in correct locations, setting up services, and so on. This will allow us to focus on the components' configuration more.

The first thing you need to do, is to add a new yum repository. The repository you need depends on your OS version, and the full list can be found at `http://www.cloudera.com/content/cloudera-content/cloudera-docs/CDH4/latest/CDH4-Installation-Guide/cdh4ig_topic_4_4.html`. All of the examples in this book will use the latest available version, CDH 4.2 on CentOS 6 64-bit. Make sure you adjust the instructions accordingly, since newer CDH versions might be available when you are reading this book. To add a repository, download this file `http://archive.cloudera.com/cdh4/redhat/6/x86_64/cdh/cloudera-cdh4.repo` and place it into `/etc/yum.repos.d/` on your server:

You will also need to add a repository GPG key:

```
# rpm --import http://archive.cloudera.com/cdh4/redhat/6/x86_64/cdh/RPM-GPG-KEY-cloudera
```

After this is done, you can check what Hadoop packages are available by running:

```
# yum search Hadoop
```

Setting up NameNode

In this section, we will do a step-by-step installation and basic configuration of the NameNode service including the High Availability (**HA**) setup. Unlike many other guides and tutorials available online, which treat NameNode's HA setup as an advanced topic, we will focus on setting up NameNode's HA from the beginning. The reason for this is the critical role NameNode plays in the Hadoop setup. Basically, NameNode is a single point of failure for Hadoop cluster. Without this service, there is no way to access files on Hadoop Distributed File System (**HDFS**).

There are several approaches to setting up NameNode High Availability. Prior to CDH 4.1, HA could be implemented using a shared storage setup. In this case, the primary NameNode writes the filesystem metadata changes into an editlog, which is located on a shared network storage, and a secondary NameNode polls changes from the editlog and applies it to its own copy of metadata snapshot. Additionally, all DataNodes updated both the NameNodes with information about the current block's location, so the secondary NameNode could take over the primary role, in the case of the primary NameNode's failure.

> Prior to CDH version 4, the secondary NameNode didn't perform a standby function. Its only role was to perform checkpoint operations. With the HA implementation, a Standby NameNode performs both HA and checkpoint functions. You can think of a Standby NameNode as a secondary NameNode + hot standby.

This setup is less than ideal. It requires additional hardware, which in turn needs to be easily available. In CDH 4.1 a new version of an easily available setup for NameNode was released, which relies on distributed services to synchronize two data nodes and eliminates the need for shared network storage. This setup is called **Quorum Journal Manager** and it introduces several new components. There are two NameNodes: primary and standby. This is similar to the previous setup, but instead of writing an editlog to the shared network file, the primary NameNode writes them to a cluster of **JournalNodes**. JournalNode is new type of daemon introduced in CDH 4.1. The idea behind JournalNodes is that the primary NameNode submits editlog changes to a group of JournalNodes, which store them on the local disks. The write is considered successful if a majority of JournalNodes are able to persist it on disk. This eliminates shared storage requirement, but still guarantees that the editlog writes are durable and there is no single point of failure. One great thing about JournalNodes is that their operations are lightweight and you don't need to run those on separate hardware.

A common practice is to run three JournalNodes (an odd number guarantees a proper quorum). Two of these can be run on the same server as NameNodes and one on a JobTracker. This is not a mandatory requirement and you can run JournalNodes on any of the servers in the cluster you choose. For our setup, we will choose this option.

Standby NameNode polls an editlog from a cluster of JournalNodes and applies them to the copy of filesystem image it has. Standby NameNode still performs the checksum function, and ships the updated fsimage file back to the primary NameNode. In addition, DataNodes are configured to send heartbeats with information about block allocation to both nodes. In the case of the primary NameNode failure, the secondary NameNode can seamlessly take over the HDFS operations.

To make the whole cross-nodes coordination possible, NameNodes rely on **ZooKeeper** to track which NameNode is primary and which one is standby, to prevent situations when both nodes decide they are primary and start writing the editlog to the JournalNodes. ZooKeeper is another Apache project, which is a part of CDH. It provides distributed coordination services and is useful when many different nodes need to share a state, locking information, or any other data information. You can find more information about ZooKeeper at http:// zookeeper.apache.org. The last piece of the NameNode HA puzzle is ZooKeeper Failover Controller (ZKFC). ZKFC is a daemon that runs on both primary and standby NameNodes, checks their health and status, and initiates a failover to a standby NameNode, if required. When it comes to dealing with NameNode failures, cluster administrators are presented with two options:

- Use **manual failover** from failed NameNode to the standby NameNode. This is a simpler setup, but it means that the cluster administrator will have to carefully monitor the health of the active NameNode and quickly initiate the failover steps if something goes wrong.

- Configure the **automatic failover** option, which relies on ZKFC to monitor the status of the active NameNode. ZKFC will initiate the failover if required and use the ZooKeeper cluster as a status synchronization point.

For our setup, we will choose the automatic NameNode failover option.

As you can see, there are many moving parts that are added with the NameNode HA setup. Here is a diagram that will help you visualize all the components involved and their relationship with each other:

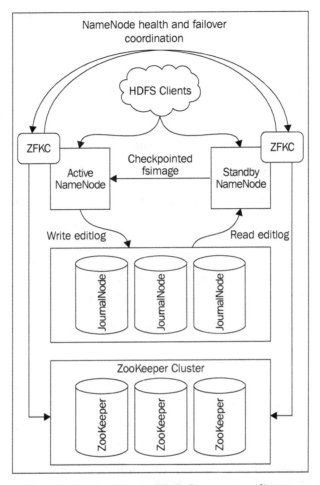

NameNode HA with JournalNode Quorum setup diagram

All of the examples in the following sections are performed on a test cluster with the following nodes being set up and configured: nn1.hadoop.test.com, nn2.hadoop.test. com, and jt1.hadoop.test.com. Names should be self-explanatory: nn1 and nn2 are primary and standby NameNodes respectively, and jt1 is a JobTracker. I will omit DataNodes for now, as we will be talking about them later in this chapter.

Dealing with a cluster of machines on a large scale, obviously, requires some degree of automation of common tasks. One of the tasks that will need to be constantly repeated while setting up and configuring a cluster is the propagation of these configuration files across different machines. Cloudera Manager can help a lot with configuration management. You can also use tools such as Puppet, Chef, or Ansible for this.

We will start with installing packages required by the NameNode on nn1, nn2, and jt1. The reason we are installing HDFS-packages on a JobTracker server is because we will need to run a JournalNode there.

> Unless specified otherwise, all commands are to be executed as a root user.

You can do it by running a simple `yum` command on nn1, nn2, and jt1 servers:

```
# yum install hadoop-hdfs-namenode
```

This will install several dependent packages. Let's quickly take a look at what those are.

- **bigtop-jsvc** and **bigtop-utils**: These packages are for the Apache Bigtop project (http://bigtop.apache.org) This project was created to help a streamline development and packaging of Hadoop components. It is responsible for proper environment setup, making sure JAVA_HOME is correctly detected in different systems, and so on. Generally, you don't have to be concerned with this but need to be aware of its existence, since some of the configuration files' locations and usages have been changed since Bigtop's introduction.
- **hadoop**: This package contains core Hadoop components, configuration files, and shared libraries. It will be installed on all cluster nodes.
- **hadoop-hdfs**: This one provides configuration files for HDFS, NameNode, JournalNode, and DataNode, built-in web-servers configurations, and so on.
- **zookeeper**: We discussed ZooKeeper's role in NameNode HA previously, but it is also being used by HBase columnar storage.

One thing to note here, is that along with the setup of HDFS packages, CDH will also create a new OS user named `hdfs`. All the daemon processes will be executed as this user.

JournalNode, ZooKeeper, and Failover Controller

The next step is to install the JournalNode package on all three servers:

```
# yum install hadoop-hdfs-journalnode
```

We have already installed the zookeeper package as a part of NameNode dependencies, but we also need to install scripts to start/stop the ZooKeeper server. Run the following command on nn1, nn2, and jt1:

```
# yum install zookeeper-server
```

And finally, we will need to install Failover Controller. This daemon needs to be executed only on primary and standby NameNodes, so we install it on nn1 and nn2:

```
# yum install hadoop-hdfs-zkfc
```

Before we can proceed with configuring NameNode and other components, we need to make sure that the ZooKeeper cluster is up and running. In our case, we have three ZooKeeper nodes on nn1, nn2, and jt1. The ZooKeeper configuration file, `zoo.cfg` is located at `/etc/zookeeper/conf/`, and here is how it looks for our setup:

```
maxClientCnxns=50
# The number of milliseconds of each tick
tickTime=2000
# The number of ticks that the initial
# synchronization phase can take
initLimit=10
# The number of ticks that can pass between
# sending a request and getting an acknowledgement
syncLimit=5
# the directory where the snapshot is stored.
dataDir=/var/lib/zookeeper
# the port at which the clients will connect
clientPort=2181

server.1=nn1.hadoop.test.com:2888:3888
server.2=nn2.hadoop.test.com:2888:3888
server.3=jt1.hadoop.test.com:2888:3888
```

The sample configuration file contains some defaults and no changes are required, unless you are doing some advanced tuning. You may need to change the `dataDir` option, depending on your setup. What needs to be added to this configuration file are the last three lines you can see in the preceding code. These lines provide a configuration for the ZooKeeper cluster. The number after each `server` word is a server ID and `2888` and `3888` are the ports for connecting to ZooKeeper and electing a new leader respectively. We don't have to be concerned with these details right now, but one thing you need to do is to double check that these ports are open on ZooKeeper nodes, and that the client port 2181 is accessible for any other servers which will need to use ZooKeeper, such as HBase nodes.

After the configuration file is updated (don't forget to update it on all the nodes!), you need to run the following command, which will create and initialize the data directory:

```
# service zookeeper-server init --myid=1
```

We have already installed the zookeeper package as a part of NameNode dependencies, but we also need to install scripts to start/stop the ZooKeeper server.

Run the following command on nn1, nn2, and jt1:

```
# yum install zookeeper-server
```

This command needs to be executed on nn1, nn2, and jt1. It will also create a file called `myid` at `/var/lib/zookeeper/` (location depends on the `dataDir` option) on all three nodes. This file contains a unique server ID for ZooKeeper nodes, and this is what you provide with the `--myid` option. So, you need to provide a different `--myid` value on each server. This is a way for the ZooKeeper daemon to understand who it is in the cluster.

To start the ZooKeeper service, execute the following command on all three nodes:

```
# service zookeeper-server start
```

Make sure you verify the contents of the log files that ZooKeeper, by default, writes at `/var/log/zookeeper/zookeeper.log`. Sometimes, even in the case of failures, the `zookeeper-server start` command still returns success, and the only way to see if the server has actually started properly is to check the log file.

Now, we are ready to proceed with the NameNode configuration.

Hadoop configuration files

Before we dive into the details of the NameNode daemon configuration, a couple of words need to be said about the Hadoop configuration files. There are many different daemons involved in a Hadoop cluster and one might expect all of them to have their own configuration files. In fact, there are only a few configuration files that you need to use for core Hadoop services. It can be confusing initially, because options for different roles are getting mixed together in several files.

There are three main configuration files for the core Hadoop components: `core-site.xml`, `hdfs-site.xml`, and `mapred-site.xml`. The `core-site.xml` file contains configuration options that are common for all servers in the cluster. The `hdfs-site.xml` and `mapred-site.xml` files provide the configuration for HDFS and MapReduce components of the cluster respectively. There are other configuration files which control different aspects of the cluster and we will take a look at those shortly. CDH puts these configuration files into the `/etc/hadoop/conf` directory, which in turn is a symbolic link to the `alternatives` directory. CDH uses the Linux Alternatives project to maintain different versions of configuration and other files. We don't have to be concerned about the exact setup, because it doesn't really affect the steps we need to take to set up a cluster.

 You can learn more about Linux Alternatives at `http://www.linuxalt.com`.

Let's take a look at what files are in `/etc/hadoop/conf` on one of our NameNode servers, nn1:

```
# ls -lh /etc/hadoop/conf
-rw-r--r--1 root root 1.2K May 21 05:40 core-site.xml
-rw-r--r--1 root root 1.8K Apr 22 19:36 hadoop-metrics2.properties
-rw-r--r--1 root root 2.5K Apr 22 19:36 hadoop-metrics.properties
-rw-r--r--1 root root 2.4K May 22 04:51 hdfs-site.xml
-rw-r--r--1 root root 8.6K Apr 22 19:36 log4j.properties
-rw-r--r--1 root root   10 Apr 22 19:36 slaves
-rw-r--r--1 root root 2.3K Apr 22 19:36 ssl-client.xml.example
-rw-r--r--1 root root 2.2K Apr 22 19:36 ssl-server.xml.example
```

You can see that `core-site.xml` and `hdfs-site.xml` are in place, but `mapred-site.xml` is missing. This is because we haven't installed any MapReduce-related packages, such as JobTracker or TaskTracker on this server yet.

The `hadoop-metrics.properties` and the `hadoop-metrics2.properties` files are controlling the way Hadoop exposes its internal metrics. This will become important when configuring cluster monitoring and we will be talking about these files in greater detail in *Chapter 5, Monitoring Hadoop Cluster*.

The `log4j.properties` configuration file is used to specify details about the Hadoop logging facilities. It is extremely flexible and allows you to specify retention and archival options, log detail level, and even log formats. Hadoop comes with a good set of defaults, so we will not discuss all available options here, but if the defaults don't fit your needs, feel free to explore the Log4j and Hadoop documentation.

The `slaves` file is optional and is empty by default. You can populate it with the list of DataNodes. This list would be used by scripts, such as `start-all.sh`, which would start all daemons in the cluster. This method of starting services in CDH is discouraged and the service command should be used instead.

The example files `ssl-client.xml.example` and `ssl-server.xml.example` are sample configuration files which can be used to set up an encrypted shuffle phase for MapReduce.

In addition to the `/etc/hadoop/conf` directory, there is another location that you need to be aware of. With the introduction of the Bigtop project, some of the settings were moved into a set of shell scripts in the `/etc/default` directory. These scripts set up some of the environment variables used by different services. Here is an example of what the default `hadoop-hdfs-namenode` script looks like (headers are stripped out to save space):

```
export HADOOP_PID_DIR=/var/run/hadoop-hdfs
export HADOOP_LOG_DIR=/var/log/hadoop-hdfs
```

```
export HADOOP_NAMENODE_USER=hdfs
export HADOOP_SECONDARYNAMENODE_USER=hdfs
export HADOOP_DATANODE_USER=hdfs
export HADOOP_IDENT_STRING=hdfs
export HADOOP_NAMENODE_OPTS="-Xmx10g"
# export HADOOP_SECURE_DN_USER=hdfs
# export HADOOP_SECURE_DN_PID_DIR=/var/run/hadoop-hdfs
# export HADOOP_SECURE_DN_LOG_DIR=/var/log/hadoop-hdfsewew
```

As you can see, this file specifies the PID and log file's location, the OS user that will be used to run the NameNode daemon, and other options. In most cases, when you implement the CDH package installation, the defaults path will be sufficient. One variable that is not part of the defaults is HADOOP_NAMENODE_OPTS. This variable specifies the list of JVM options that will be used for starting up the NameNode daemon. In this case, the NameNode JVM will be started with a maximum heap size of 10 GB. You will need to adjust your configuration based on the estimates of the number of files/blocks that you plan to store in HDFS. For details on RAM requirements for the NameNode please refer to *Chapter 1, Setting Up Hadoop Cluster – from Hardware to Distribution*.

NameNode HA configuration

We will start configuring our NameNode HA setup by adding several options to the core-site.xml file. The following is the structure of the file for this particular step. It will give you an idea of the XML structure, if you are not familiar with it. The header comments are stripped out:

```
<?xml version="1.0"?>
<?xml-stylesheet type="text/xsl" href="configuration.xsl"?>
<configuration>
<property>
    <name>fs.default.name</name>
    <value>hdfs://sample-cluster/</value>
</property>
<property>
    <name>ha.zookeeper.quorum</name>
    <value>nn1.hadoop.test.com:2181,nn2.hadoop.test.com:2181,
       jt1.hadoop.test.com:2181
    </value>
</property>
</configuration>
```

The configuration file format is pretty much self-explanatory; variables are surrounded by the <property> tag, and each variable has a name and a value.

There are only two variables that we need to add at this stage. `fs.default.name` is the logical name of the NameNode cluster. The value `hdfs://sample-cluster/` is specific to the HA setup. This is the logical name of the NameNode cluster. We will define the servers that comprise of it in the `hdfs-site.xml` file. In a non-HA setup, this variable is assigned a host and a port of the NameNode, since there is only one NameNode in the cluster.

The `ha.zookeeper.quorum` variable specifies locations and ports of the ZooKeeper servers. The ZooKeeper cluster can be used by other services, such as HBase, that is why it is defined in `core-site.xml`.

The next step is to configure the `hdfs-site.xml` file and add all HDFS-specific parameters there. I will omit the `<property>` tag and only include `<name>` and `<value>` to make the list less verbose.

```
<name>dfs.name.dir</name>
<value>/dfs/nn/</value>
```

NameNode will use the location specified by the `dfs.name.dir` variable to store the persistent snapshot of HDFS metadata. This is where the fsimage file will be stored. As discussed previously, the volume on which this directory resides needs to be backed by RAID. Losing this volume means losing NameNode completely. The `/dfs/nn` path is an example, however you are free to choose your own. You can actually specify several paths with a `dfs.name.dir` value, separating them by commas. NameNode will mirror the metadata files in each directory specified. If you have a shared network storage available, you can use it as one of the destinations for HDFS metadata. This will provide additional offsite backups.

```
<name>dfs.nameservices</name>
<value>sample-cluster</value>
```

The `dfs.nameservices` variable specifies the logical name of the NameNode cluster and should be replaced by something that makes sense to you, such as `prod-cluster` or `stage-cluster`. The value of `dfs.nameservices` must match the value of `fs.default.name` from the `core-site.xml` file.

```
<name>dfs.ha.namenodes.sample-cluster</name>
<value>nn1,nn2</value>
```

Here, we specify the NameNodes that make up our HA cluster setup. These are logical names, not real server hostnames or IPs. These logical names will be referenced in other configuration variables.

```
<name>dfs.namenode.rpc-address.sample-cluster.nn1</name>
<value>nn1.hadoop.test.com:8020</value>
```

```
<name>dfs.namenode.rpc-address.sample-cluster.nn2</name>
<value>nn2.hadoop.test.com:8020</value>
```

This pair of variables provide mapping from logical names like nn1 and nn2 to the real host and port value. By default, NameNode daemons use port 8020 for communication with clients and each other. Make sure this port is open for the cluster nodes.

```
<name>dfs.namenode.http-address.sample-cluster.nn1</name>
<value>nn1.hadoop.test.com:50070</value>

<name>dfs.namenode.http-address.sample-cluster.nn2</name>
<value>nn2.hadoop.test.com:50070</value>
```

Each NameNode daemon runs a built-in HTTP server, which will be used by the NameNode web interface to expose various metrics and status information about HDFS operations. Additionally, standby NameNode uses HTTP calls to periodically copy the fsimage file from the primary server, perform the checkpoint operation, and ship it back.

```
<name>dfs.namenode.shared.edits.dir</name>
<value>qjournal://nn1.hadoop.test.com:8485;nn2.hadoop.test.
com:8485;jt1.hadoop.test.com:8485/sample-cluster</value>
```

The `dfs.namenode.shared.edits.dir` variable specifies the setup of the JournalNode cluster. In our configuration, there are three JournalNodes running on nn1, nn2, and nn3. Both primary and standby nodes will use this variable to identify which hosts they should contact to send or receive new changes from editlog.

```
<name>dfs.journalnode.edits.dir</name>
<value>/dfs/journal</value>
```

JournalNodes need to persist editlog changes that are being submitted to them by the active NameNode. The `dfs.journalnode.edits.dir` variable specifies the location on the local filesystem where editlog changes will be stored. Keep in mind that this path must exist on all JournalNodes and the ownership of all directories must be set to `hdfs:hdfs` (user and group).

```
<name>dfs.client.failover.proxy.provider.sample-cluster</name>
<value>org.apache.hadoop.hdfs.server.namenode.ha.ConfiguredFailoverPro
xyProvider</value>
```

In an HA setup, clients that access HDFS need to know which NameNode to contact for their requests. The `dfs.client.failover.proxy.provider.sample-cluster` variable specifies the Java class name, which will be used by clients for determining the active NameNode.

At the moment, there is only `ConfiguredFailoverProxyProvider` available.

```
<name>dfs.ha.automatic-failover.enabled</name>
<value>true</value>
```

The `dfs.ha.automatic-failover.enabled` variable indicates if the NameNode cluster will use a manual or automatic failover.

```
<name>dfs.ha.fencing.methods</name>
<value>sshfence
        shell(/bin/true)
</value>
```

Orchestrating failover in a cluster setup is a complicated task involving multiple steps. One of the common problems that is not unique to the Hadoop cluster, but affects any distributed systems, is a "split-brain" scenario. Split-brain is a case where two NameNodes decide they both play an active role and start writing changes to the editlog. To prevent such an issue from occurring, the HA configuration maintains a marker in ZooKeeper, clearly stating which NameNode is active, and JournalNodes accepts writes only from that node. To be absolutely sure that the two NameNodes don't become active at the same time, a technique called fencing is used during failover. The idea is to force the shutdown of the active NameNode before transferring the active state to a standby.

There are two fencing methods currently available: `sshfence` and `shell. sshfence`. These require a passwordless ssh access as a user that starts the NameNode daemon, from the active NameNode to the standby and vice versa. By default, this is the hdfs user. The fencing process checks if there is anyone listening on a NameNode port using the `nc` command, and if the port is found busy, it tries to kill the NameNode process. Another option for `dfs.ha.fencing.methods` is shell. This will execute the specified shell script to perform fencing. It is important to understand that failover will fail if fencing fails. In our case, we specified two options, the second one always returns success. This is done for workaround cases where the primary NameNode machine goes down and the ssh method will fail, and no failover will be performed. We want to avoid this, so the second option would be to failover anyway, even without fencing, which, as already mentioned, is safe with our setup. To achieve this, we specify two fencing methods, which will be tried by ZKFC in the order of: if the first one fails, the second one will be tried. In our case, the second one will always return success and failover will be initiated, even if the server running the primary NameNode is not available via ssh.

```
<name>dfs.ha.fencing.ssh.private-key-files</name>
<value>/var/lib/hadoop-hdfs/.ssh/id_rsa</value>
```

The last option we will need to configure for NameNode HA setup is the ssh key, which will be used by sshfence. Make sure you change the ownership for this file to hdfs user. Two keys need to be generated, one for the primary and one for the secondary NameNode. It is a good idea to test ssh access as an hdfs user in both directions to make sure it is working fine.

The `hdfs-site.xml` configuration file is now all set for testing the HA setup. Don't forget to sync these configuration files to all the nodes in the cluster. The next thing that needs to be done is to start JournalNodes. Execute this command on nn1, nn2, and jt1 a root user:

```
# service hadoop-hdfs-journalnode start
```

With CDH, it is recommended to always use the service command instead of calling scripts in `/etc/init.d/` directly. This is done to guarantee that all environment variables are set up properly before the daemon is started. Always check the logfiles for daemons.

Now, we need to initially format HDFS. For this, run the following command on nn1:

```
# sudo -u hdfs hdfs namenode -format
```

This is the initial setup of the NameNode, so we don't have to worry about affecting any HDFS metadata, but be careful with this command, because it will destroy any previous metadata entries. There is no strict requirement to run format command on nn1, but to make it easier to follow, let's assume we want nn1 to become an active NameNode. Format command will also format the storage for the JournalNodes.

The next step is to create an entry for the HA cluster in ZooKeeper, and start NameNode and ZKFC on the first NameNode. In our case, this is nn1:

```
# sudo -u hdfs hdfs zkfc -formatZK
# service hadoop-hdfs-namenode start
# service hadoop-hdfs-zkfc start
```

Check the ZKFC log file (by default, it is in `/var/log/hadoop-hdfs/`) to make sure nn1 is now an active NameNode:

```
INFO org.apache.hadoop.ha.ZKFailoverController: Trying to make
NameNode at nn1.hadoop.test.com/192.168.0.100:8020 active...
INFO org.apache.hadoop.ha.ZKFailoverController: Successfully
transitioned NameNode at nn1.hadoop.test.com/192.168.0.100:8020 to
active state
```

To activate the secondary NameNode, an operation called bootstrapping needs to be performed. To do this, execute the following command on nn2:

```
# sudo -u hdfs hdfs namenode -bootstrapStandby
```

This will pull the current filesystem state from active NameNode and synchronize the secondary NameNode with the JournalNodes Quorum.

Now, you are ready to start the NameNode daemon and the ZKFC daemon on nn2. Use the same commands that you used for nn1. Check the ZKFC log file to make sure nn2 successfully acquired the secondary NameNode role. You should see the following messages at the end of the logfile:

```
INFO org.apache.hadoop.ha.ZKFailoverController: ZK Election indicated
that NameNode at nn2.hadoop.test.com/192.168.0.101:8020 should become
standby
INFO org.apache.hadoop.ha.ZKFailoverController: Successfully
transitioned NameNode at nn2.hadoop.test.com/192.168.0.101:8020 to
standby state
```

This is the last step in configuring NameNode HA. It is a good idea to verify if automatic failover is configured correctly, and if it will behave as expected in the case of a primary NameNode outage. Testing failover in the cluster setup stage is easier and safer than discovering that failover doesn't work during production stage and causing a cluster outage. You can perform a simple test: kill the primary NameNode daemon and verify if the secondary takes over its role. After that, bring the old primary back online and make sure it takes over the secondary role.

> You can use execute the following command to get the current status of NameNode nn1:
>
> ```
> # sudo -u hdfs hdfs haadmin -getServiceState nn1
> ```
>
> The `hdfs haadmin` command can also be used to initiate a failover in manual failover setup.

At this point, you have a fully configured and functional NameNode HA setup.

JobTracker configuration

Like NameNode, JobTracker plays a master role in the MapReduce framework; it collects heartbeat messages from TaskTrackers in the cluster, maintains information about the cluster's current capacity and is responsible for scheduling, submitting, and progress tracking of user-defined jobs. This is a lot of work to do and on a large cluster, JobTracker can become very busy; but unlike NameNode, JobTracker has to maintain much less state information about running jobs, and besides, when maintaining job logs there are minimal requirements for persistent storage.

For a long time, JobTracker, just like NameNode, was a single point of failure in a Hadoop cluster. If the JobTracker process fails, all currently running or scheduled jobs will fail and have to be restarted. Until the release of CDH 4.1, it was the user's responsibility to monitor the job status and re-submit it in case of JobTracker failures. In CDH 4.1, first steps towards high availability were made and the job persistence feature was added to the JobTracker. Now, JobTracker can automatically restart all the jobs that were running during the JobTracker crash or restart. In CDH 4.2, JobTracker's High Availability setup was introduced. It allows for configuring active and standby JobTrackers and performing automatic failover if the active JobTracker fails. One thing you need to be aware of when configuring JobTracker HA is that all jobs that were running at the moment of failover will have to be restarted from the beginning on the standby JobTracker. JobTracker HA setup uses similar components for the NameNode HA setup. It uses ZooKeeper to store information about which node is currently active, and relies on ZKFC daemons to monitor JobTracker's health and perform automatic failover. JobTrackers will share the job status information via files on HDFS, so no additional storage cluster, such as JournalNodes, is required.

For our sample installation, we will not be using JobTracker HA, but we will configure the job status information persistence. There are several reasons for setting things up this way. First of all, JobTracker HA is not as critical as NameNode HA. The Daemon process restarts or unplanned server reboots can be easily tolerated with jobs being automatically restarted by JobTracker upon startup. In the case of a complete server failure, it is easy enough to set up a new JobTracker, since no previous state information is required to make JobTracker operational quickly. So, JobTracker HA doesn't provide much when it comes to daemon crashes and restarts, but it can shorten recovery time in case of catastrophic node failure. It is up to you to decide where JobTracker is important for your cluster, depending on the SLAs you may have for the jobs running there. The second reason why JobTracker HA will not be discussed in detail is because setting it up is similar in many aspects to NameNode HA; you will need to configure a logical name for the JobTracker cluster, describe both servers participating in it in the configuration file, set up ZKFC, and so on.

You should be able to quickly configure HA for JobTracker by following the CDH HA guide, which can be found at `http://www.cloudera.com/content/cloudera-content/cloudera-docs/CDH4/latest/CDH4-High-Availability-Guide/cdh4hag_topic_3.html`

To install the JobTracker package, execute the following command on the dedicated server. In our sample cluster, the JobTracker hostname is `jt1.hadoop.test.com`:

```
# yum install hadoop-0.20-mapreduce-jobtracker
```

This command will install `hadoop-0.20-mapreduce` as a dependent package, which actually contains all the relevant `.jar` files, and other related files. The JobTracker package only provides default files and a server startup script. You should start seeing the trend, in the way things are packaged, by now.

MapReduce specific parameters are stored in `/etc/hadoop/conf/mapred-site.xml`, which is used by both JobTracker and TaskTracker. A small quirk of the JobTracker package is that it doesn't provide a skeleton configuration file, so you should create it manually.

The first thing we need to configure is a JobTracker hostname and port. This option will be used by TaskTrackers to know where to look for master node:

```
<name>mapred.job.tracker</name>
<value>jt1.hadoop.test.com:8021</value>
```

As mentioned previously, local disk space requirements for JobTracker are minimal. Besides the standard log files, JobTracker also stores configurations for all the submitted user jobs as well as historical information on completed jobs. This logging goes to the standard Hadoop log directory, which, in CDH, is located at `/var/log/hadoop-0.20-mapreduce/`. Additionally, JobTracker needs to store some of its system information on the local disk. This data is not critical and normally doesn't take much disk space. The following variable specifies the location of this local directory:

```
<name>mapred.local.dir</name>
<value>/tpm/mapred/jt</value>
```

The `mapred.local.dir` directory needs to be owned by the mapred user and group. This is the user that CDH created during the package installation.

MapReduce jobs need to run on a large number of machines, so there is a need to be able to propagate job shared files, as job configuration files, jar files, among others to all of them. JobTracker uses HDFS to store such files. It allows shared files to be easily accessed by TaskTrackers on all cluster nodes.

The following variable specifies the location of such a shared directory:

```
<name>mapred.system.dir</name>
<value>/tmp/mapred/system</value>
```

There is no real indication of whether the paths in the `mapred-site.xml` file are referring to the local filesystem, or are using HDFS, so it's important to remember which variables are responsible for what.

MapReduce also writes some information about the running and completed jobs into HDFS, so users who are submitting jobs can easily access it. To make this happen, the following variable needs to point to the root user directory, which is normally `/user` in HDFS:

```
<name>mapreduce.jobtracker.staging.root.dir</name>
<value>/user</value>
```

The next couple of variables are related to how the job status information is stored on HDFS. Previously, JobTracker stored the job status information in memory, so in the case of a daemon restart, there was a possibility that MapReduce clients would never get the status of their submitted jobs. To fix this issue, Job Status Store was created, which is basically a directory in HDFS. To activate Job Status Store, you need to enable the following variables:

```
<name>mapred.job.tracker.persist.jobstatus.active</name>
<value>true</value>
```

By default, job status information will be written to the `/jobtracker/jobsInfo` directory on HDFS. You can control this location with the `mapred.job.tracker.persist.jobstatus.dir` variable. We will use a default for our setup, so we need to create these directories in HDFS and set proper permissions:

```
# sudo -u hdfs hdfs dfs -mkdir /jobtracker
# sudo -u hdfs hdfs dfs -chown mapred:mapred /jobtracker
```

The next variable allows restarting of the jobs that were running when JobTracker was restarted or crashed. JobTracker reads the job status from HDFS and restarts it. While it can provide an additional level of reliability and allow resuming failed jobs faster than the case where human interaction is required, you should decide if this option is required in your cluster. There are several potential issues that can occur with this automatic job restart. First of all, some clients may decide to restart jobs themselves, in the case of a failure, and this leads to a situation where multiple copies of the same job are submitted. In a multitenant environment, the general rules regarding job submissions can be hard to impose.

Another potential problem is that JobTracker crashes can be actually related to the jobs that are currently running, and restarting all the jobs after JobTracker is back online, without proper investigation about what caused the crash, may not be the best idea. On the other hand, if you have a good level of control of jobs that are running on the cluster, or you have strict SLAs around jobs completion, enabling automatic jobs restart is a valid option.

```
<name>mapred.jobtracker.restart.recover</name>
<value>true</value>
```

You can also control for how long the job status information is being stored in HDFS by setting the following option:

```
<name>mapred.job.tracker.persist.jobstatus.hours</name>
<value>24</value>
```

Configuring the job scheduler

One of the main roles of JobTracker is to schedule user jobs and submit them to the TaskTrackers. There is probably no Hadoop cluster for production purposes out there that is being used to run one job at a time. In most of the cases, there will be several jobs submitted by different users and a valid question of how the cluster resources will be allocated for competing jobs. From the MapReduce framework's perspective, cluster capacity consists of available map and reduce slots. These parameters are defined during TaskTrackers' configuration and are a fixed number for each worker node. TaskTrackers send regular messages to the JobTracker with the information of how many map and reduce slots are currently occupied on a given server, and it is a responsibility of a JobTracker scheduler to decide how to utilize those slots in the most efficient way.

There are several algorithms that JobTracker can use to schedule concurrent jobs. These algorithms are implemented as pluggable classes and need to be specified in the `mapred-site.xml` file. It is the responsibility of the administrator to choose the best scheduler for a given workload. Scheduler is identified by the `mapred.jobtracker.taskScheduler` variable, which is a Java class name for a specific scheduler. At the moment, there are three different schedulers available: JobQueueTaskSchedule, FairScheduler, and CapacityTaskScheduler. Since achieving good cluster utilization is a top priority for any Hadoop administrator, it is worth giving a brief overview of the main differences between schedulers.

JobQueueTaskScheduler

The default, most primitive scheduler, is JobQueueTaskSchedule or FIFO scheduler. This scheduler forms a queue of submitted jobs, and lets the first job arrive and occupy all available slots in the cluster. All other jobs will have to wait in the queue for the first job to finish completely. This can cause significant wait times, even for small jobs if they are unlucky to get scheduled after a long job. Such an approach is less than optimal in environments where long ETL processes have to co-exist with short-lived user requests. FIFO scheduler allows assigning different priorities to the jobs that are submitted, but each priority level just gets assigned to a separate queue, and jobs from a high priority queue are getting submitted to the TaskTrackers faster than jobs from a lower priority queue. This scheduler lacks important features of a proper resource manager and is not a good fit for most production installations.

FairScheduler

The second available scheduler is FairScheduler. The main idea behind FairScheduler is to allow equal distribution of cluster resources to different jobs over a period of time. Jobs are organized into pools, where each pool gets an equal amount of cluster slots. By default, FairScheduler is configured to create a pool per user, but other options are also available. If there is only one job running, it is allowed to consume all available slots, but slots that are freed (some map tasks will finish faster than others) can be re-used by other jobs. There is also a way to assign a minimal amount of cluster resources' shares to more important pools. For example, you may want to do it for critical production jobs. You can also configure this scheduler to kill running tasks to guarantee adequate capacity for high priority jobs. FairScheduler provides much better cluster utilization for multitenant environments and has more advanced tuning options. We will choose this scheduler for our cluster configuration.

CapacityTaskScheduler

The last currently available scheduler is CapacityTaskScheduler. This scheduler uses an approach similar to FairScheduler, but with some differences. Jobs are assigned into a pre-defined set of queues and each queue gets a portion of cluster resources specified by the administrator. This share of resources is assigned to a queue and is not given away, even if there are no other jobs running. Inside a queue, jobs are scheduled in a FIFO fashion, meaning that jobs from one user will be serialized within a queue. One of the interesting features of CapacityTaskScheduler is that this scheduler can interpret information about system resources utilization such as RAM, reported by TaskTrackers and make scheduling decisions based on general server utilization and not only by looking at the cluster slots available. This is a popular option for production usage and works well when the type of load is more or less static.

As mentioned earlier, we will configure FairScheduler for our sample setup. We will use a basic setup with the task pool created for each user and all pools configured with no minimal capacity sharing requirements. First of all, we need to specify the scheduler we want to use:

```
<name>mapred.jobtracker.taskScheduler</name>
<value>org.apache.hadoop.mapred.FairScheduler</value>
```

Next, we need to configure how pools will be created. In the following example, each user submitting a job will get a separate pool:

```
<name>mapred.fairscheduler.poolnameproperty</name>
<value>user.name</value>
```

The value of the `mapred.fairscheduler.poolnameproperty` variable can be any job property. For example, to create a pool based on the user's primary OS group, you can set the value to `group.name`.

An administrator can pre-define pools in a separate XML file called the `allocations` file. All the additional pool properties such as minimal slots shared, are specified in this file. For our setup, we will allow FairScheduler to dynamically create pools for every user submitting a job, with no additional options. To do this, create a new file in `/etc/hadoop/conf/` and name it `fair-scheduler.xml`. It will be an empty XML file with only one section in it:

```
<?xml version="1.0"?>
<allocations>
</allocations>
```

Now, we need to specify the location of this file in `mapred-site.xml`:

```
<name>mapred.fairscheduler.allocation.file</name>
<value>/etc/hadoop/conf/fair-scheduler.xml</value>
```

Since we haven't declared any pools, we need to allow FairScheduler to allocate pools dynamically. This is done by setting the `mapred.fairscheduler.allow.undeclared.pools` variable to true:

```
<name>mapred.fairscheduler.allow.undeclared.pools</name>
<value>true</value>
```

If you would like to fine tune the pools' behavior, you can explore the available options in the scheduler documentation at `http://hadoop.apache.org/docs/r1.2.1/fair_scheduler.html`.

These are the all JobTracker configuration options we need to specify at this stage. You can now start the daemon using the service command:

```
# service hadoop-0.20-mapreduce-jobtracker start
```

DataNode configuration

Now that we have finished configuring Hadoop master services, NameNode and JobTracker, it's time to configure nodes where most of the data processing is done: the DataNodes.

DataNodes are Hadoop's worker nodes, they also comprise the majority of the cluster's server population. DataNodes play a dual role; they host the DataNode HDFS daemon, as well as the TaskTracker from the MapReduce framework. This blend allows the MapReduce jobs to utilize locality of data and avoid expensive network transfers when possible.

Let's walk through the details of DataNode configuration. You then will be able to replicate these steps across all DataNodes in your cluster. For the following examples, I have added a new host to the sample cluster: dn1.hadoop.test.com. The same assumptions we made for NameNode installation are true for this section as well. Local disk volumes should be properly formatted and mounted, OS tuning applied, there should be no firewall restrictions for Hadoop ports, and the CDH repository should be configured.

To install a DataNode using the CDH package, use the following yum command:

```
# yum install hadoop-hdfs-datanode.x86_64
```

This will install Hadoop core, Hadoop HDFS, and DataNode specific packages. Actually, the `hadoop-hdfs-datanode` package includes only the default configuration file and service startup script. All the core components are being installed as a part of hadoop and hadoop-hdfs packages.

Now, we need to add several DataNode specific options into `hdfs-site.xml`. Some of these options are used by DataNode exclusively, some of them can be used by different HDFS clients, but to keep things consistent we will edit the `hdfs-site.xml` file, which we already have, after we finish the NameNode configuration and propagate it on all the nodes in the cluster.

First, we need to specify which volumes DataNode will use to store actual HDFS data. This is done by setting the `dfs.data.dir` variable:

```
<name>dfs.data.dir</name>
<value>
```

```
/dfs/data1,/dfs/data2,/dfs/data3,/dfs/data4,/dfs/data5,/dfs/data6
</value>
```

This variable is a comma-separated list of volumes that are local on each DataNode. Since no RAID is usually configured for DataNodes, these volumes are actually separate disks. DataNode will use these disks in a round-robin fashion to store the HDFS data.

The next variable we add to `hdfs-site.xml` is `dfs.block.size`. This variable sets the default block size in bytes for files that are stored in HDFS. You can override this setting by specifying the block size for a given file. By default, Hadoop uses a 64 MB block size, and these days in most production installations a 128 MB block size has became the standard. You can vary the block size for different files, when you upload them into HDFS by specifying a client-side option. If no such option is provided, Hadoop will use `dfs.block.size` from the configuration file. For our sample cluster, we will go with a 128 MB block size:

```
<name>dfs.block.size</name>
<value>134217728</value>
```

Another core variable that controls HDFS behavior is `dfs.replication`. This variable specifies how many times each file block will be replicated. The default setting is 3 and in most cases, this is the optimal choice between cluster resilience and total usable cluster storage capacity. Just like with block size, HDFS clients can specify a replication factor on a per file basis. Even though there is no need to adjust this variable, it's a good idea to explicitly add it to the configuration file to make it easy to understand which setting is used:

```
<name>dfs.replication</name>
<value>3</value>
```

There are two other variables related to `dfs.replication`, the `dfs.replication.max` variable, that limits the number of possible replicas of one block in the cluster. By default, it's `512`. You may want to lower this value if you don't trust all the clients that are using your cluster, and if you don't want anyone to flood the filesystem with files setup to replicate 512 times. Another related setting is `dfs.namenode.replication.min`. It controls what would be the minimal number of replicas for a given block to consider the block write completed. The default for this variable is `1`, which means if at least one DataNode stored the block, the write operation is considered successful. Such default behavior means that some files will be stored with a number of replicas less than those demanded by the dfs.replication setting. This can happen when there is a network issue in the cluster or not all DataNodes are available.

Hadoop will periodically scan the filesystem for such under-replicated blocks and will try to replicate them to match with the system default. The default of 1 is a reasonable setting for the `dfs.namenode.replication.min` and we will leave it as it is for our setup, but you may want to review this setting, especially if you have strong requirements for data resilience.

The next variable that we will specify for DataNode configuration is `dfs.du.reserve`. The name of this variable is not very descriptive, but the idea is that Hadoop can reserve some space on the disks that are being used by DataNodes. This is required because the MapReduce framework will need a local volume to store temporary data. Both the map and reduce phase of the jobs will generate temporary files, and having enough space in the MapReduce temporary directory is critical. It's a common practice to utilize the same local disks that HDFS uses to be able to split the IO load across multiple spindles, but this means that some space needs to be reserved to prevent a situation where all the disk space is consumed by HDFS, and MapReduce jobs start failing because there is nowhere to transfer temporary data to. It's a good idea to reserve about 10 percent of the total disk capacity on each disk, unless you plan to have a dedicated volume on each server for the MapReduce temporary directory. To reserve 10 GB per disk, we will use the following setting:

```
<name>dfs.du.reserve</name>
<value>10737418240</value>
```

Before we start the DataNode daemon, it is worth double checking the JVM heap settings. By default, DataNode will start with 1 GB heap memory size. It is enough in most cases, because DataNode is mostly focused on large sequential reads and writes, but if you need to adjust it, use the `/etc/default/hadoop-hdfs-datanode` file and set the `HADOOP_DATANODE_OPTS` variable, similar to what we did for the NameNode's heap size:

```
export HADOOP_DATANODE_OPTS="-Xmx1024m"
```

Now, we are ready to start the DataNode daemon using the `service` command:

```
# service hadoop-hdfs-datanode start
```

Always check logfiles for the daemons that were just started, especially when making changes to the configuration files. If DataNode started successfully and was able to communicate with the active and standby NameNode, you should see messages in the log file indicating that DataNode started sending block allocation information to the NameNodes.

To verify that DataNode is functioning properly, we will perform two simple tests. It is possible to use HDFS at this point, even though we have configured only one DataNode. Recall the `dfs.namenode.replication.min` setting. With a default value of 1, HDFS will be able to store files, if at least one replica of file blocks can be created. This will allow us to verify the configuration on one DataNode before investing time into propagating these settings across all DataNodes.

First of all, we will create a temporary directory in HDFS and then upload a sample file there. A temporary directory in Hadoop plays the same role as a /tmp directory in your Linux installation. Some of the ecosystem projects that we will be setting up in further chapters will require /tmp to be present in HDFS. To create a new directory in HDFS, we will use the `hdfs` command:

```
# sudo -u hdfs hdfs dfs -mkdir /tmp
```

The `hdfs` command-line client tool is used to perform various operations on HDFS. It accepts HDFS commands as arguments and generally tries to mimic standard Linux commands such as `mkdir`, `ls`, `rm`, among others. Note that we execute this command as an hdfs user because we need to create a root level directory in the filesystem and hdfs is an equivalent of a root user for your local filesystem. If you try to execute this command as a root user, you will get a permission denied error.

Now, we need to set permissions on the /tmp directory in HDFS, in the same fashion you would do for the local filesystem; everyone is allowed to write and read to this directory, but users can only delete or rename their own files (sticky bit). There is a `chmod` command for HDFS which is similar to the following Linux command:

```
# sudo -u hdfs hdfs dfs -chmod 1777 /tmp
```

Let's create a simple text file, `test.txt` and upload it into HDFS, assuming the file is in /root you can upload it using the following command:

```
# hdfs dfs -put /root/test.txt /tmp
```

To verify that the file was correctly loaded we can use the `-ls` and `-cat` commands for hdfs. You can also use the `hdfs fsck` command to verify the health of the filesystem.

At this point, you should proceed with configuring the rest of the DataNodes in your cluster. Obviously, when dealing with a large number of machines, using automation tools to propagate configuration files and execute commands in parallel comes in handy.

TaskTracker configuration

TaskTracker is the final piece of the Hadoop core that we need to set up and configure. TaskTracker is to MapReduce framework what DataNode is to HDFS. TaskTrackers are responsible for launching and executing individual tasks for the jobs that JobTracker submits to them. TaskTrackers' daemons run on the same servers as DataNodes. This is required to maximize local data access during the map phase. JobTracker is smart enough to figure out on which DataNodes, the file blocks—that will be required by individual tasks—reside, and submit those tasks to TaskTrackers running on the same server.

First of all, we need to install the required packages:

```
# yum install hadoop-0.20-mapreduce-tasktracker
```

Similarly to JobTracker, the `hadoop-0.20-mapreduce` package will be installed as a dependency.

The TaskTracker daemon uses the same `mapred-site.xml` configuration file, just as JobTracker does. This may not be the best decision, because some settings may have different values for TaskTracker and JobTracker. In the following examples, we will assume that you maintain two different versions of `mapred-site.xml`, one for JobTracker and one for all TaskTrackers.

The first setting we need to specify is the address and port of the JobTracker daemon:

```
<name>mapred.job.tracker</name>
<value>jt1.hadoop.test.com:8021</value>
```

This is exactly the same value we configured for JobTracker too.

We have also configured `mapred.local.dir` on the JobTracker server as well, but on TaskTracker, it has a different function. While it still specifies local volumes to store temporary data, requirements for local storage are more demanding on TaskTracker. MapReduce jobs will use this local storage to save temporary data (map task output data), which later will be passed to the reduce phase. The size of the data and intensity of IO can be significant, depending on the types of jobs you run and jobs concurrency. A common practice is to allocate separate directories for the jobs' data on the same disks that DataNodes are using. This allows for enough disk space, as well as utilizing multiple disks to improve IO throughput. Previously, we have configured the `dfs.du.reserve` variable for the DataNode daemon. This is required to prevent HDFS hogging up all the disk space and causing jobs to fail, because they can't write to a temporary location anymore. We configured the same variable on JobTracker, but disk space requirements there are much humbler. Here is how to configure this variable on TaskTracker:

```
<name>mapred.local.dir</name>
<value>
/dfs/data1/mapred,/dfs/data2/mapred,/dfs/data3/mapred,
/dfs/data4/mapred,/dfs/data5/mapred,/dfs/data6/mapred
</value>
```

This assumes that your HDFS volumes are mounted on `/dfs/data*`. Make sure that a mapred OS user can access the mapred directories.

TaskTracker is where the Hadoop cluster capacity configuration happens. From MapReduce's perspective, cluster capacity consists of available map slots and available reduce slots. The number of slots that each TaskTracker will be available to allocate depends on the server hardware configuration, specifically, the CPU and RAM available. Creating more slots that a single worker node can handle doesn't make much sense, because then the job processes will start to compete for machine resources, causing significant slowdown. Let's assume we are setting up a smaller cluster of higher-end machines with 16 CPU cores and 64 GB of RAM per node, as discussed earlier. The rule of thumb is to approximately match the number of available slots with the number of available cores. For faster servers, oversubscribing the CPU a little bit is OK and for a 16 core machine, we can allocate a total of 24 task slots (16 * 1.5 = 24). Keep in mind that these are the *total* available slots, including map and reduce slots, since map tasks do initial data processing and one map task is created for each input split, you can expect that there will be more demand for map slots than for reduce slots. The reduce phase is executed over data that map tasks produce and is generally expected to process much less data than the map phase did. The exact ratio of an available map to reduce slots will depend on the actual workload, but a good starting point would be to allocate 2/3 of all server slots to map tasks and 1/3 to reduce tasks. For our 16 core machine, we will have 16 map slots and 8 reduce slots:

```
<name>mapred.tasktracker.map.tasks.maximum</name>
<value>16</value>
<name>mapred.tasktracker.reduce.tasks.maximum</name>
<value>8</value>
```

TaskTracker creates separate Java processes for each map and reduce tasks, so apart from its own heap memory settings, it needs to provide those settings to the child processes as well. Just like with all other Hadoop daemons we have configured so far, TaskTracker's heap size can be configured by setting the HADOOP_TASKTRACKER_OPTS variable in the `/etc/default/hadoop-0.20-mapreduce` file:

```
export HADOOP_TASKTRACKER_OPTS="-Xmx1G"
```

The default setting for the TaskTracker heap memory is 1G and it should be enough for most installations. This setting, though, is not related to the memory that will be available to map and reduce processes. For this, a `mapred.java.child.opts` variable in `mapred-site.xml` is used. Actually, it can be used to provide different parameters to map and reduce processes, but the most common are minimum and maximum heap memory settings. The amount of RAM that you should allocate to individual tasks depends on the total number of slots configured and the server RAM. For our example, for a server that has 64 GB of RAM and a total of 24 task slots, allocating 2G per task is reasonable:

```
<name>mapred.java.child.opts</name>
<value>-Xmx2G</value>
```

The `mapred.java.child.opts` variable is just an option string that will be passed to the task processes, so you can include additional options, such as the amount of memory that will be allocated to the process initially with the `-Xms` option.

This concludes the basic TaskTracker configuration and we are now ready to start it. Use the following command to bring it online:

```
service hadoop-0.20-mapreduce-tasktracker
```

Check the TaskTracker log file to make sure there are no errors. Typical problems during initial setup are caused by incorrect permissions on local directories, typos in JobTracker address, and so on. You can also run the following command to list all TaskTrackers that have successfully registered with JobTracker:

```
# hadoop job -list-active-trackers
```

Before you propagate this setup to all the TaskTrackers, we run a final validation test and that is executing an actual MapReduce job. This will be a basic WordCount example, that is often presented as a "Hello, World" equivalent for MapReduce. It is also included in examples shipped with CDH packages.

1. First of all, create a file with some arbitrary text in it and save it in a local directory. Let's assume you are doing it on the jt1 server and operating as a root user. To execute a MapReduce job, you need to create a `/user/root` directory in HDFS. It will be used as a job staging directory. Make sure the ownership is assigned to the root:

   ```
   # sudo -u hdfs hdfs dfs -mkdir /user/root
   # sudo -u hdfs hdfs dfs -chown root:root /user/root
   ```

2. Note that we are performing these operations as an hdfs user, which is a superuser for HDFS, while the root from HDFS' perspective is just an ordinary user. Next, create a job input directory in /user/root:

```
# hdfs dfs -mkdir /user/root/words_input
```

3. To upload a file into HDFS, use the following command:

```
# hdfs dfs -put /tmp/words.txt /user/root/words_input
```

4. The word count example, along with other sample jobs is located in /usr/lib/hadoop-0.20-mapreduce/hadoop-examples.jar. To submit a MapReduce job, use the hadoop jar command:

```
# hadoop jar /usr/lib/hadoop-0.20-mapreduce/
hadoop-examples.jar wordcount /user/root/words_input
 /tmp/words_output
```

5. The hadoop jar command takes in several arguments: the location of the .jar file, the class name of the job we want to run, the directory where to look for input files, and the directory where to write the final results. The output directory is getting created for every job run, so make sure it doesn't exist before you start the job. If everything is configured properly after executing this command, you should see the job execution progress and some additional statistics, including the time spent in map and reduce phases, the number of rows processed, and so on.

6. Take a look at the output directory, you should see the following files:

```
# hdfs dfs -ls /user/root/words_output
Found 3 items
-rw-r--r--   3 root supergroup          0 /user/root/words_
output/_SUCCESS
drwxrwxrwt   - root supergroup          0 /user/root/words_
output/_logs
-rw-r--r--   3 root supergroup         65 /user/root/words_output
part-r-00000
```

7. The _SUCCESS file is a marked file, indicating the job completed without errors. The _logs directory contains the job execution logs, and finally part-r-00000 is the result file containing words and their respective counts from the input file. You can check its content by running this command:

```
# hdfs dfs -cat /user/root/words_output/part-r-00000
```

If everything worked as described here, your MapReduce and HDFS configurations are valid and you can proceed with propagating them across all nodes in the cluster.

Advanced Hadoop tuning

The previous sections described the steps to set up and configure core Hadoop components. After you learn more about your typical production workload and the types of job that are being executed, you may want to adjust some of the additional configuration settings to improve or balance the workload better. Hadoop exposes much more configuration options than what we have already discussed. You will probably never need to change most of them, but there are a few performance related variables worth being mentioned here.

hdfs-site.xml

NameNode needs to respond to many different requests from HDFS clients, including DataNodes and external applications. To handle those requests efficiently, NameNode spawns several threads to handle this load and the number of threads it creates is configurable via the `dfs.namenode.handler.count` variable. The default number of threads is `10`, but if you are setting up a large cluster you may want to increase it. There are different opinions on how to calculate this number, but generally you will not get a significant performance boost from setting this value too high. Set this value to `100` if your cluster size exceeds 200 nodes, and to `50` if it is less than that:

```
<name>dfs.namenode.handler.count</name>
<value>50</value>
```

Adding new DataNodes to the cluster to increase the total capacity, or to replace the failed nodes, is a common task that the Hadoop administrator will need to perform sooner or later. While new nodes will start accepting blocks for newly created files and replicas, existing data will not be rebalanced automatically. This means that your new node will not be fully utilized. To force Hadoop to move existing data blocks to servers that have lots of capacity, you need to run the `hdfs balancer` command, but moving terabytes of data across the network can easily disrupt regular jobs. To prevent this, Hadoop throttles balancing data moves to a value defined in the `dfs.datanode.balance.bandwidthPerSec` variable, which is in bytes per second. The exact value will depend on the network bandwidth in your cluster; the default is 1 MB/sec. To increase it to 10 MB/sec, use the following setting:

```
<name>dfs.datanode.balance.bandwidthPerSec</name>
<value>10485760</value>
```

mapred-site.xml

Similar to the NameNode, JobTracker can get pretty busy responding to multiple client requests. To make sure JobTracker has enough threads allocated for this purpose, you need to tune the `mapred.job.tracker.handler.count` variable. Use the same rule as for the NameNode threads number:

```
<name>mapred.job.tracker.handler.count</name>
<value>50</name>
```

MapReduce's jobs' performance is highly influenced by the sort-and-shuffle phase, when the output of an individual map task has to be sorted by keys, merged together into several larger files, and sent to reducers. This phase normally generates a lot of network traffic and can also cause significant local IO. When a map task needs to sort its output, it uses an internal buffer and once this buffer is full, it spills data onto local disks. To reduce the number of such spills you can increase the value of the `io.sort.mb` variable. By default, it is set to `100 MB` and it is a good buffer size for most of the workloads. If you are observing a lot of local IO during the sort phase, you can increase this value. To increase the sort buffer to 200 MB, add the following lines to the `mapred-site.xml` file:

```
<name>io.sort.mb</name>
<value>200</value>
```

 Keep in mind that this buffer is allocated as a part of the task's heap size, specified by the `mapred.java.child.opts` variable.

A related option is `io.sort.factor`. It specifies how many files will be merged in one batch. Again, there is no strict rule about this variable, but the default of `10` seems to be too low. You can start with `32`, which is a somewhat arbitrary number, and observe the cluster's performance to tune it further:

```
<name>io.sort.factor</name>
<value>32</value>
```

During the reduce phase of the jobs map, the outputs, belonging to a given key range, need to be copied to a specific reducer. There can be many such pieces scattered across the cluster, and to speed up the copy reducers use several parallel processes. By default, there are five copy processes created in parallel. You may want to increase this value if you are setting up a large cluster, or you plan to run jobs that will need thousands of map tasks. For small to medium sized clusters (20-100 nodes) go with 12-16 parallel processes:

```
<name>mapred.reduce.parallel.copies</name>
<value>12</value>
```

core-site.xml

Large Hadoop clusters are spawn across multiple racks in datacenters, but it is not unusual to see smaller clusters to be split between two or three different racks. For smaller clusters, the multiple rack setup provides additional redundancy in case one of the racks fails. Hadoop was designed to be rack-aware, for example, being able to make some optimizations, depending on which rack a given server belongs to. One of such optimizations is a block replica placement strategy that Hadoop uses. It will try to store at least one replica in a different rack to increase data resilience. When requesting data blocks for, say, a MapReduce job, Hadoop will try to minimize cross-rack network traffic, picking up servers that are in the same rack instead.

To be able to use this feature, Hadoop needs to know which server belongs to which rack. The idea is that a Hadoop administrator will provide an executable, which will return a rack ID and server IP or hostname. The implementation of this executable is completely up to the administrator. The most common case is to create a comma-separated text file, which will keep the server mapped to the racks, and write a shell / python / perl script, which will take an IP or hostname as an argument and return the rack ID. The rack ID can be any string. Providing such a script is beyond the scope of this book, but there are multiple versions available online. To enable rack-awareness, you need to specify your script path in the `net.topology.script.file.name` variable:

```
<name>net.topology.script.file.name</name>
<value>/etc/Hadoop/conf/rack_topology.bash</value>
```

If no script is provided, Hadoop assumes that all servers are within one rack.

Summary

This chapter provides step-by-step guidelines for setting up and configuring core Hadoop components. We have started with identifying what are the most critical OS settings that need to be adjusted for a Hadoop server. Then, we focused on steps to set up NameNode, DataNode, JobTracker, and TaskTracker using CDH distribution for CentOS Linux distribution. To eliminate a single point of failure for HDFS, we have configured a NameNode High Availability cluster using JournalNodes Quorum. Following these steps you can build a fully functional, production-ready cluster. Hadoop core components are enough to start performing useful work, but over time, lots of ecosystem projects have evolved around Hadoop. Some of them became a must-have cluster component. We will enrich our cluster with additional functionality provided by those projects in the next chapter, *Configuring the Hadoop Ecosystem*.

3
Configuring the Hadoop Ecosystem

Hadoop is a powerful distributed data processing system. The cluster which we configured in the previous chapter is a ready-to-use system, but if you start using Hadoop in this configuration for any real-life applications, you will very soon discover that MapReduce provides a very low-level way to access and process the data. You will need to figure out lots of things on your own. You will need to decide how to export data from external sources and upload it into Hadoop in the most efficient way. You will need to figure out what format to store data in and write the Java code to implement data processing in the MapReduce paradigm. The Hadoop ecosystem includes a number of side projects that have been created to address different aspects of loading, processing, and extracting data. In this chapter, we will go over setting up and configuring several popular and important Hadoop ecosystem projects:

- Sqoop for extracting data from external data sources
- Hive for high-level, SQL-like access to data
- Impala for real-time data processing

There are many more Hadoop related projects, but we will focus on those that will instantly improve the Hadoop cluster usability for end users.

Hosting the Hadoop ecosystem

Often, additional Hadoop components are not hosted within the cluster itself. Most of these projects act as clients to HDFS and MapReduce and can be executed on separate servers. Such servers were marked as Hadoop clients, as shown in the cluster diagram from *Chapter 1, Setting Up Hadoop Cluster – from Hardware to Distribution*. The main reason for separating Hadoop nodes from clients physically and on a network level is security. Hadoop client servers are supposed to be accessed by different people within your organization. If you decide to run clients on the same servers as Hadoop, you will have to put in lots of effort providing a proper level of access to every user. Separating those instances logically and physically simplifies the task. Very often, Hadoop clients are deployed on virtual machines, since resource requirements are modest.

 Keep in mind those clients who read and write HDFS data need to be able to access NameNodes, as well as all DataNodes in the cluster.

If you are running a small cluster or have a limited number of users and are not too concerned with security issues, you can host most of the client programs on the same nodes as NameNodes or DataNodes.

Sqoop

Sqoop is a tool, which connects two worlds: relational databases and Hadoop. Importing data from relational databases into Hadoop and the other way around is a very common task. For many organizations, Hadoop is a data integration platform. Let's imagine you have lots of application logfiles produced by your website. These logs have very valuable information about how users interact with your application, but the only user information you can capture in logs is the username. On the other hand, you have a very detailed user profile data in your relational database. Being able to easily export this data into Hadoop and perform some analysis on how different classes of users interact with a website is extremely important. On the other hand, results produced by complex long running MapReduce jobs can be relatively small in size. Very often this data is loaded into RDBMS for real-time data access or integration with BI tools.

Installing and configuring Sqoop

Sqoop is a command-line tool, though future versions will provide a client-server type of access. Sqoop is almost always deployed on the servers outside the Hadoop cluster.

Sqoop needs to be able to access all the Hadoop nodes, as well as relational databases that you plan to use. It is easier to provide such a level of access only to a few selected Sqoop nodes.

It is easy to install Sqoop using the CDH repository:

```
# yum install sqoop
```

If you are installing it on a client server, where no CDH packages were yet installed, you will need to install several dependencies, including Hadoop-client and Hadoop-MapReduce packages.

The Sqoop package comes with several configuration files:

```
# ls -lh /etc/sqoop/conf/
-rwxr-xr-x 1 root root 1.4K Apr 22 20:38 sqoop-env-template.sh
-rwxr-xr-x 1 root root 5.0K Apr 22 20:38 sqoop-site-template.xml
-rwxr-xr-x 1 root root 5.0K Apr 22 20:38 sqoop-site.xml
```

The template files provide a list of options that you can use to tune Sqoop. Fortunately, if you are using CDH distribution, you will not need to change lots of things there. The main Sqoop configuration file `sqoop-site.xml` comes with a good set of defaults and Sqoop can work right out of the box. There are several options related to the Metastore configuration that you may want to change. We will discuss them later.

Sqoop relies on JDBC drivers to connect to different database servers. These drivers are not shipped with Sqoop due to licensing differences and have to be installed separately. To demonstrate the basic import/export functionality of Sqoop, we will use a MySQL database as a source. You can download the MySQL JDBC driver from `mysql.com`. The driver comes in a form of a `.jar` file and needs to be copied under `/usr/lib/sqoop/lib` to be picked up by Sqoop automatically.

Sqoop import example

For the following examples, we will use the MySQL "world" database, which can be found at `http://dev.mysql.com/doc/index-other.html`. To execute the examples, you need to have the MySQL server up and running, load the `world` database into it, create a user for Sqoop, and make sure that the machine running Sqoop can access the remote (or local) MySQL server.

To import a table from MySQL into Hadoop, you can run the following command:

```
# sqoop import --connect jdbc:mysql://mysql-db.server.example.com/world
--table Country --username sqoop_user -P
Enter password:
```

The options that are passed to Sqoop in this case are pretty straightforward. We need to specify the JDBC connection string, the table that we want to import (Country in this case), and the MySQL user, we have created for this purpose. You can also specify which JDBC driver to use using the --driver option. Keep in mind that JDBC connection string formats vary between databases, so always refer to the database documentation.

It is important to understand how Sqoop performs the import. Sqoop analyzes the table that you are trying to import and generates a Java MapReduce code to be executed on a Hadoop cluster. Each map task will connect to the MySQL database, read a portion of the data using SELECT statements, and write it into HDFS. Sqoop is trying to utilize the parallelism that Hadoop provides, to speed up the import process. This is great for performance, but one needs to keep in mind some implications of such an approach. One of the most important implications is the fact that import tasks are running from several cluster servers and are completely independent from the database perspective. This means that there is no transactional consistency guaranteed. You can control the number of parallel tasks with the --num-mappers option, which is 4, by default.

 Be careful when using the --num-mappers option. It is easy to overload your database with too many concurrent connections coming from multiple Hadoop nodes.

Let's take a look at the files that got imported. By default, Sqoop will create a new directory in the HDFS home directory of the user running the job. The new directory name will match the table name that is being imported. You can control the destination directory with the --warehouse-dir option. Here is what you will see if you check your HDFS home directory after the import (output stripped for brevity):

```
# hdfs dfs -ls /user/alice/Country
Found 6 items
0 2013-06-05 20:56 /user/alice/Country/_SUCCESS
0 2013-06-05 20:54 /user/alice/Country/_logs
9919 2013-06-05 20:56 /user/alice/Country/part-m-00000
6990 2013-06-05 20:56 /user/alice/Country/part-m-00001
7069 2013-06-05 20:56 /user/alice/Country/part-m-00002
7512 2013-06-05 20:56 /user/alice/Country/part-m-00003
```

The _SUCCESS and _logs files should be familiar to you from the Wordcount MapReduce program that we ran in *Chapter 2, Installing and Configuring Hadoop*. This shows very clearly that each Sqoop import is, in fact, a MapReduce job. You will also notice that there are four result files. This is because there were 4 separate map tasks used for this import. Each of them generated a separate plain text file. You can now inspect those files using the hdfs command, run MapReduce jobs over them, and so on.

Sqoop export example

To demonstrate the reverse process of loading data into MySQL (or any other relational database), create a sample CSV file and save it into HDFS /user/alice/tomysql directory:

```
# hdfs dfs -cat /user/alice/tomysql/result
```

To export data into a MySQL table, run the following command:

```
# sqoop export --connect jdbc:mysql://mysql-db.server.example.com/test
--table hadoop_results --username sqoop_user -P --export-dir /user/root/
tomysql/
```

This is not very different from the import command. Here, we need to specify which MySQL table will be used for data load with the --test option and from where Sqoop will read the data with --export-dir. After the job is finished, you can verify if the data was properly loaded using the simple SELECT statement.

These examples only show very basic operations that Sqoop can perform. Sqoop is much more flexible and powerful than what was demonstrated. It allows for controlling which data will be imported from relational databases using custom conditions. Sqoop can perform incremental imports, keeping track of what rows were already imported. You can specify which file formats and compression types to use and much more. Detailed documentation on Sqoop can be found at http://sqoop.apache.org/docs/1.4.3/SqoopUserGuide.html.

 The new version of Sqoop 2 will address several limitations of the current version. This includes running in client-server mode, providing reusable database connections, having a proper permissions model, and so on. As of now, Sqoop 2 still doesn't have a stable release.

Hive

If you were curious to explore the source code of the WordCount MapReduce job example from *Chapter 2, Installing and Configuring Hadoop*, or tried to write some code yourself, you should have realized by now that this is a very low-level way of processing data in Hadoop. Indeed, if writing MapReduce jobs was the only way to access data in Hadoop, its usability would be pretty limited.

Hive was designed to solve this particular problem. It turned out, that lots of MapReduce code that deal with data filtering, aggregation, and grouping can be generated automatically. So, it is possible to design a high-level data processing language, which can then be compiled into native Java MapReduce code. Actually, there is no need to design a new language for this. SQL has been a de facto standard for processing data in relational databases. For Hive developers, the solution was obvious: take a SQL dialect and build Hive as a compiler from SQL to MapReduce. The language that Hive provides is called **HiveQL**. It is worth mentioning that projects like Pig took a different course and instead of re-using SQL as a high-level language, they came up with a new language of their own.

The ability to utilize SQL on a Hadoop cluster dramatically increases its usability and widens the community of users who can work with the cluster data. It also allows integrating applications that use a SQL-interface with Hadoop. This makes Hive one of the must-have components in the Hadoop ecosystem.

Hive architecture

Essentially, Hive performs the following tasks: take a HiveQL query, compile it into a MapReduce task, submit this task to the cluster, and present the results back to the user. To compile HiveQL into MapReduce code, Hive has to understand the structure of the data that is being queried. Hive organizes data into familiar relational tables, which have columns of defined types. On the other hand, Hive operates on data stored in the Hadoop cluster and Hadoop doesn't impose any schema on its data, as you already know. This means that Hive has to provide an additional layer to store the metadata for its table. Hive implements this layer via the **Metastore** service.

Metastore is a two-component service. The first component is a server accepting connections from Hive clients and providing them with information about the tables that they need. The second one is a relational database that Metastore uses to persist the metadata on disk. Hive Metastore supports several databases for this purpose, such as MySQL, PostgreSQL, and Oracle. MySQL is a popular choice for the Metastore backend and we will use it for our cluster. Metastore can operate in different modes. You can use Metastore embedded with the Hive client.

You can run Metastore as a local service and connect several Hive clients to it. Or, you can run a remote cluster-wide service, which can be used by multiple clients from many machines. There are use cases for all options, but for production Hadoop clusters, running a remote Metastore is the most common choice. This way you can easily share the Hive metadata among multiple clients, while isolating clients from a backend relational database. You can also run multiple Metastore servers for high availability purposes.

So far, when we mentioned the Hive client, we actually meant the Hive command-line interface. The SQL-like interface allows Hive to support applications that use JDBC and ODBC drivers. This makes the Hive query engine and data available to a wide range of third-party applications. These applications don't communicate with Metastore directly, but rely on a **Hive Server** that provides query compilation and Metastore access services.

If you refer to the Hadoop cluster diagram from *Chapter 1, Setting Up Hadoop Cluster – from Hardware to Distribution* once again, you will see that we have allocated a separate server for Hive Metastore and other services. We will stick to the plan and install Hive Metastore, Hive Server, and the Metastore backend database on a separate machine. This is optional and you may choose to colocate these servers with other Hadoop components, such as JobTracker or NameNode. Hardware resources requirements for Hive are modest, but will depend on the number of clients and the Hive table that you plan to host.

Installing Hive Metastore

Before we install Hive Metastore, we need to make sure that there is a backend database up and running. For our cluster, we will use the MySQL database for this purpose. We will run the MySQL database on the same server on which Hive Metastore runs, but often the backend database is located outside the Hadoop cluster. Installing and configuring MySQL is beyond the scope of this book. You can refer to `http://dev.mysql.com/doc/refman/5.5/en/installing.html` for MySQL installation details. It is worth mentioning that losing Hive metadata can have a big impact, since you will need to recreate all the table definitions. Setting up proper HA and backups for the Metastore backend database is important.

After MySQL is installed and configured, you need to create a MySQL database and a user for Hive Metastore.

If you have configured the CDH repository on the Hive Metastore server, as described in *Chapter 2, Installing and Configuring Hadoop*, you can now simply use the following `yum` command to install Metastore:

```
# yum install hive-metastore
```

Hive configuration is similar to other Hadoop components. Configuration files, including template files with all options and their descriptions, are located under /etc/hive/conf. There are many configuration options available, but we will focus on the core ones to get Hive up and running quickly. All options should be added to the hive-site.xml file.

> You need to copy the hdfs-site.xml and mapred-site.xml files from Hadoop cluster nodes into the /etc/Hadoop/conf directory on all Hive-related servers. Otherwise, Hive will not be able to communicate with HDFS and launch MapReduce jobs.

First of all, we need to specify which database driver to use for the backend. In our case, we need to add the following property:

```
<name>javax.jdo.option.ConnectionDriverName</name>
<value>com.mysql.jdbc.Driver</value>
```

Several options provide credentials to the backend database and are self-explanatory, so we will just include them in one block, as follows:

```
<name>javax.jdo.option.ConnectionURL</name>
<value>jdbc:mysql://localhost/hive_meta </value>

<name>javax.jdo.option.ConnectionUserName</name>
<value>hivemetauser</value>

<name>javax.jdo.option.ConnectionPassword</name>
<value>secret</value>
```

The database connection string has a simple JDBC format and the MySQL user and password should match those created during the MySQL installation.

As mentioned earlier, you can run several Metastore services, using the same database backend for High Availability purposes. You need to specify the connection string for all those Metastores in the hive.metastore.uris variable. In our case, there is only one Metastore:

```
<name>hive.metastore.uris</name>
<value>thrift://hive.hadoop.test.com:9083</value>
```

In the preceding code, hive.hadoop.test.com is the hostname of the machine running Metastore and 9083 is the default port it is listening on. You can change the port by modifying the PORT variable in the /etc/default/hive-metastore file. Make sure this port is available to all Hive clients.

Finally, we need to specify where Hive will store the tables' data. In Hive, every database and table is represented by a directory and a set of files in HDFS. You can specify what would be a default location for these files with the `hive.metastore.warehouse.dir` variable:

```
<name>hive.metastore.warehouse.dir</name>
<value>/warehouse</value>
```

To start Metastore service, we need to take the following steps:

1. The Hive warehouse directory needs to be created in HDFS with appropriate permissions. Run the following command as an `hdfs` user:

   ```
   # hdfs dfs -mkdir /warehouse
   # hdfs dfs -chmod a+w /warehouse
   ```

2. Note that we are allowing all users to write to the `/warehouse` directory. This is important to allow multiple users to use Hive. Another approach is to assign all Hive users to one group and change the `/warehouse` ownership to this group.

3. Download and install the MySQL JDBC driver. It is not shipped with Hive packages, due to license differences, so you need to download it from `http://dev.mysql.com/downloads/connector/j/`. After unpacking the archive, copy the `.jar` file to the Hive `lib` directory using the following command:

   ```
   # cp mysql-connector-java-5.1.25-bin.jar /usr/lib/hive/lib/
   ```

4. Start Hive Metastore using the following command:

   ```
   # service hive-metastore start
   ```

Always check error log files to confirm that the service has actually started properly. By default, Hive log files can be found in the `/var/log/hive` directory.

Installing the Hive client

In this section, we will install Hive CLI and link it to Hive Metastore. Hive clients can be installed on any machine inside the cluster, but in most cases they are installed on dedicated Gateway servers. Normally, you, as a Hadoop administrator, will need to provide Hive client access to multiple users inside your organization. Isolating these users on Gateway machines makes it much easier to control and manage these permissions.

To install the Hive client, run the following command:

```
# yum install hive
```

Like in the case of Hive Metastore, you will need to copy the Hadoop configuration files to the client machines, to provide Hive access to HDFS and MapReduce.

The Hive client uses the same configuration file `hive-site.xml` as Metastore does. You will not need to copy the Metastore configuration file to the clients, though. The whole idea of Metastore is to encapsulate access to the backend database. Hive clients don't need to have access to the MySQL database, which we have configured for Metastore. Only Hive Metastore needs to have MySQL credentials specified in its configuration file.

Instead, you will use a separate Hive client configuration file. Fortunately, there are only a few core options required to get Hive up and running.

First of all, you need to specify that you are going to use remote Metastore. Add the following option into `hive-site.xml` on your Hive client servers:

```
<name>hive.metastore.local</name>
<value>false</value>
```

Next, you need to point Hive clients to the location of Hive Metastore:

```
<name>hive.metastore.uris</name>
<value>thrift://hive.hadoop.test.com:9083</value>
```

These two options are enough for the Hive client to operate. To launch Hive CLI, run the following `hive` command:

```
# hive
Logging initialized using configuration in file:/etc/hive/conf.dist/hive-
log4j.properties
Hive history file=/tmp/root/hive_job_log_88a7e774-cdb5-4d6c-b1eb-
77ad36207a91_1397164153.txt
hive>
```

You can see some information about Hive log files being printed on the screen. Log files' levels and locations can be adjusted in the `hive-log4j.properties` file.

You can refer to the Hive documentation at the following website for details on creating Hive tables, writing HiveQL queries, and so on: `https://cwiki.apache.org/confluence/display/Hive/Tutorial`

Installing Hive Server

At this point, you should have Hive Metastore and Hive clients installed and configured. This setup is enough if you are only planning to use Hive CLI, but if you need to provide access to applications using Hive JDBC or ODBC drivers, you need to install and configure Hive Server. Such applications may include advanced web interfaces to Hive, such as Beeline and BI tools. This will also allow you to access Hive from programs in Python, Perl, and other languages.

We will install Hive Server on the physical machine that we used for Hive Metastore, though this is not a requirement. You can install Hive Server on any other machine in the cluster.

There are two versions of Hive Server currently available in the CDH repository: HiveServer1 and HiveServer2. We will install HiveServer2, because it provides concurrent clients' support, additional security options, and some other improvements. HiveServer2 is where all the new development is happening and HiveServer1 is included in the repository for compatibility purposes.

To install HiveServer2, run the following command:

```
# yum install hive-server2
```

If you look into the package content, you will notice that it only provides scripts for the server startup/shutdown. All the required binaries were already installed with Hive and Hive Metastore packages.

There are several options, which you need to add to the `/etc/hive/conf/hive-site.xml` file for the HiveServer2 support. First, we need to enable concurrent clients' support:

```
<name>hive.support.concurrency</name>
<value>true</value>
```

HiveServer2 uses the ZooKeeper cluster to manage table locks, which is required for proper concurrency management. We will point it to the ZooKeeper server, which we have configured in *Chapter 2, Installing and Configuring Hadoop* for NameNode HA:

```
<name>hive.zookeeper.quorum</name>
<value>nn1.hadoop.test.com:2181,nn2.hadoop.test.com:2181,jt1.hadoop.
test.com:2181</value>
```

Since we are installing HiveServer2 on the same machine as Hive Metastore, we are using the same configuration file. If you decide to install HiveServer2 on a separate machine, you need to point it to Metastore using the `hive.metastore.uris` option.

By default, HiveServer2 will use port `10000`, but you can control this by changing the `HIVE_PORT` option in the `/etc/defaults/hive-server2` file.

You can now start HiveServer2 by running the following command:

```
# service hive-server2 start
```

Impala

Impala is a new member of the Hadoop ecosystem. Its beta version first became available in 2012 and the first stable release was done in June 2013. Even though Impala is a new project and still has lots of things that need to be improved, the significance of the goal that it is trying to achieve makes it worth mentioning in this book. Impala's goal is very ambitious — bringing real-time queries to Hadoop. Hive made it possible to use a SQL-like language to query data in Hadoop, but it was still limited by the MapReduce framework when it comes to performance. It is worth mentioning that projects like Stinger (`http://hortonworks.com/labs/stinger/`) are dedicated to significantly improve Hive performance, but it is still in development.

Impala bypasses MapReduce and operates on the data directly in HDFS to achieve significant performance improvements. Impala is written mostly in C++. It uses RAM buffers to cache data and generally operates more like parallel relational databases. Impala was designed to be compatible with Hive. It uses the same HiveQL language and even utilizes existing Hive Metastore to get information about tables and columns. If you have existing Hive tables in your cluster, you will be able to query them with Impala without any changes.

Impala architecture

Impala comprises of several components. There is an **Impala server** process, which should be running on each DataNode in the cluster. Its responsibility is to process queries from clients, read and write data into HDFS, perform join and aggregation tasks, and so on. Since queries are executed in parallel on many servers, the daemon that received the user request becomes a query coordinator and synchronizes the work of all other nodes for this particular query.

As DataNodes in Hadoop cluster or individual Impala daemons can go down from time to time, there is a need to keep a constant track of the state of all daemons in the cluster. For this purpose, Impala uses an **Impala state store**. If some of the Impala servers do not report back to the state store, they get marked as dead and are excluded for further queries attempts. Impala servers can operate without a state store, but the response may be delayed if there are failed nodes in the cluster.

Additionally, Impala utilizes the same Metastore service that we have configured for Hive in the *Installing Hive Metastore* section. Impala provides both, a command-line interface and JDBC/ODBC access.

There are no additional hardware requirements for Impala services. Impala servers are always running on DataNodes, because they rely on local data access. Impala state store can be co-located with existing Hadoop services, such as JobTracker or standby NameNode.

Installing Impala state store

For our cluster, we will install state store on the JobTracker node. Impala is not included in the standard CDH repository, so you will need to add a new repository by copying the `http://archive.cloudera.com/impala/redhat/6/x86_64/impala/cloudera-impala.repo` file into the `/etc/yum.repos.d/` directory on all Hadoop nodes, except NameNodes.

 The link to the Impala repository may change. Please refer to the Cloudera documentation at the following website for up-to-date information: `http://www.cloudera.com/content/cloudera-content/cloudera-docs/Impala/latest/Installing-and-Using-Impala/ciiu_prereqs.html`

Once this is done, you can install Impala state store by running the following `yum` command:

```
# yum install impala-state-store
```

State store package contains only startup scripts and Impala binaries will be installed as part of dependent impala packages.

The state store doesn't require much configuration. Impala doesn't pick up existing Hadoop configuration files, but relies on HDFS for data access. This means that you will need to manually copy the `core-site.xml` and `hdfs-site.xml` files from your Hadoop configuration directory into `/etc/imala/conf` directory.

You can adjust the state store port and logging directory by editing the `/etc/default/impala` file. By default, state store uses port `24000`. We will keep it as it is.

To start state store, run the following command:

```
# service impala-state-store start
```

You need to check the log file in `/var/log/impala` to make sure the service has started properly.

Installing the Impala server

To install the Impala server on DataNodes, run the following command:

```
# yum install impala-server
```

This will install Impala binaries, as well as the server start stop script. Before we can start the Impala server, some additional tuning needs to be applied to the DataNode configuration.

Impala uses an HDFS feature called short circuit reads. It allows Impala to bypass the standard DataNode level and be able to read file blocks directly from the local storage. To enable this feature, you need to add the following options to the `hdfs-site.xml` file:

```
<name>dfs.client.read.shortcircuit</name>
<value>true</value>

<name>dfs.domain.socket.path</name>
<value>/var/run/hadoop-hdfs/dn._PORT</value>
```

Local HDFS clients like Impala will use the socket path to communicate with DataNode. You need to leave the value of `dfs.domain.socket.path` as it is shown here. Hadoop will substitute it with the DataNode port number.

Additionally, Impala will try and track the location of file blocks independently from DataNodes. Previously, the NameNode service was only able to provide information about which block resides on which server. Impala takes this one step further and keeps track of which file blocks are stored on which disk for this DataNode. To do that, a new API was introduced in CDH 4.1. To enable it, you need to add the following options to the `hdfs-site.xml` file:

```
<name>dfs.datanode.hdfs-blocks-metadata.enabled</name>
<value>true</value>

<name>dfs.client.file-block-storage-locations.timeout</name>
<value>3000</value>
```

You will need to apply the preceding changes on all DataNodes and restart DataNodes daemons before you can proceed with the Impala configuration.

The next thing that we need to do is to point the Impala server to the state store, which we have configured on our JobTracker earlier. To do that, change the following variables in the `/etc/default/impala` configuration file:

```
IMPALA_STATE_STORE_HOST=jt1.hadoop.test.com
IMPALA_STATE_STORE_PORT=24000
```

Impala is a very memory-intensive process. Currently, it has to perform operations such as table joins completely in memory. If there is not enough memory available, the query will be aborted. Additionally, Impala will need to cache metadata about existing tables, files, and blocks' locations. To control the upper limit of Impala memory allocation, add the `-mem_limit=X` option to the `IMPALA_SERVER_ARGS` variable in `/etc/default/impala`. X will be the percentage of the available physical RAM on the server.

To properly allocate resources for both MapReduce tasks and Impala queries, you need to know what are your cluster workload profiles. If you know that there will be a MapReduce job running concurrently with Impala queries, you may need to limit the Impala memory to 40 percent of the available RAM, or even less. Be prepared that some Impala queries will not be able to complete in this case. If you are planning to use Impala as a primary data-processing tool, you can allocate as much as 70-80 percent of RAM to it.

The Impala server, as well as the Impala state store does not re-use existing Hadoop configuration files. Before you start the Impala server, you need to copy the `core-site.xml` and `hdfs-site.xml` files into the `/etc/impala/conf` directory.

To start the Impala server, run the following command:

```
# service impala-server start
```

To use Impala in a command line, you will need to install the Impala command-line interface:

```
# yum install impala-shell
```

To launch the Impala shell, execute the following command:

```
# imapla-shell
```

To connect to the Impala server, run the following command in the Impala shell:

```
> connect dn1.hadoop.test.com;
Connected to dn1.hadoop.test.com:21000
Server version: impalad version 1.0.1 RELEASE (build
df844fb967cec8740f08dfb8b21962bc053527ef)
```

 Keep in mind, that currently Impala doesn't handle automatic metadata updates. For example, if you have created a new table using Hive, you will need to run a REFRESH command in Impala shell to see the changes.

You now have a fully functional Impala server running on one of your DataNodes. To complete the installation, you need to propagate this setup across all your DataNodes. Each Impala server can accept client requests from shell or applications. The server, which received the requests, becomes a query coordinator, so it is a good idea to distribute requests equally among the nodes in the cluster.

Impala is still in the active development phase. Make sure you check the documentation for every new release, because many aspects of the Impala configuration and general behavior may change in future.

Summary

In this chapter, we learned to install three major Hadoop ecosystem projects. Sqoop, Hive, and Impala significantly increased the usability of the cluster. There are many more Hadoop ecosystem projects that we can't cover in this book. Most of them are available in CDH repositories, so you can install them when required. In the next chapter, we will cover Hadoop security options. Companies trust their most critical and sensitive data to Hadoop, so it is important to understand how to make this data secure and safe.

4
Securing Hadoop Installation

In this chapter, we will look into the essential topics related to Hadoop security. As you know, Hadoop consists of multiple components and securing a Hadoop cluster means securing each of those components. This makes securing a Hadoop cluster a nontrivial task. In this chapter, we will cover the following topics:

- Hadoop security overview
- HDFS security
- MapReduce security
- Hadoop Service Level Authorization
- Hadoop and Kerberos

Hadoop security overview

Originally, Hadoop was designed to operate in a trusted environment. It was assumed that all cluster users can be trusted to correctly present their identity and will not try to obtain more permissions than they have. This resulted in implementation of a **simple security mode**, which is the default authentication system in Hadoop. In a simple security mode, Hadoop trusts the operating system to provide the user's identity. Unlike most relational databases, Hadoop doesn't have any centralized users and privileges storage. There is no user/password concept that would allow Hadoop to properly authenticate the user. Instead, Hadoop accepts the name of the user as represented by the operating system and trusts it without any further checks. The problem with this model is that it is possible to impersonate another user. For example, a rogue user could use a custom built HDFS client, which instead of using Java calls to identify the current OS user will just substitute it with the root user and gain full access to all the data. The simple security mode can still be a preferred choice in some cases, especially if the cluster is in a trusted environment and there are only a few users having access to the system.

For many organizations, such a relaxed approach to user authorization is not acceptable. Companies are starting to store sensitive data in their Hadoop clusters and are concerned with being able to isolate data in large multitenant environments. To solve this problem, Hadoop introduced support for **Kerberos**. Kerberos is a proven authentication protocol. The Kerberos server is used as an external user's repository, which allows users to authenticate with a password. Users that have successfully authenticated with Kerberos are granted an **access ticket.** They can use the Hadoop services while this ticket is valid. Kerberos support is introduced not only for external cluster users, but for all internal services as well. This means that all DataNode, TaskTracker, NameNode, and so on daemons need to authenticate with Kerberos before they can join the cluster. Kerberos provides a much stronger security mode for Hadoop, but it also introduces additional challenges in terms of configuration and maintenance of the cluster.

HDFS security

HDFS mimics the Unix-style filesystem permissions mode. Each file and directory has a user, group owner, and set of permissions. These permissions can allow or disallow user access to a given directory or file. For example:

```
# hdfs dfs -ls /
drwxr-xr-x   - mapred mapred        0 2013-05-27 04:40 /jobtracker
drwxrwxrwt   - hdfs   supergroup    0 2013-06-08 16:03 /tmp
```

You can see that the /jobtracker directory is owned by the user mapred and only this user is allowed to write files into this directory, while every user can read files in this directory. On the other hand, while the /tmp directory is owned by the hdfs user, everyone can read and write files there. This mimics the behavior of the Unix-type /tmp directory.

 Note that there is a sticky bit set on the /tmp directory as well. This will allow only the file owner to delete and rename files there.

To manipulate files permissions, HDFS provides commands that are similar to those of the Unix environment. As an example, let's create a home directory for the user alice and change the directory ownership:

```
[root@nn1 ~]# hdfs dfs -mkdir /user/alice/
mkdir: Permission denied: user=root, access=WRITE, inode="/
user":hdfs:hdfs:drwxr-xr-x
```

This attempt to create a directory fails and we get an error because the Linux root user doesn't have appropriate permissions on HDFS.

In CDH, the `hdfs` user is an equivalent of `superuser` —a user with the highest level of privileges. This is because all the HDFS daemons are running under the `hdfs` user.

 It is important to distinguish the user "hdfs" from the hdfs command line tool.

To fix this error, we will switch to the `hdfs` user instead:

```
# sudo su - hdfs
$ hdfs dfs -mkdir /user/alice/
$ hdfs dfs -chown alice:alice /user/alice/
```

You can also use the `-chmod` command with syntax similar to the syntax in Linux, to change the access mode for files and directories.

 There is no direct connection between OS users and the permissions you assign on HDFS. When you change the directory or file ownership, Hadoop doesn't check if the user actually exists. You need to be careful with the correct spelling of the usernames, since you will not get **user doesn't exist** errors from HDFS.

MapReduce security

MapReduce security is focused around jobs submission and administration. By default, it is wide open. Any user who has access to the JobTracker service can submit, view, and kill jobs. Such behavior can be acceptable for the development or POC clusters, but obviously fails for the multitenant production environment.

To address these problems, Hadoop supports the notion of **cluster administrator** and **queue administrators**. Cluster and queue administrators are Linux users and groups that have permissions to see and manipulate running jobs. Administrators could, for example, change job priority or kill any running job.

If you recall, in *Chapter 2, Installing and Configuring Hadoop*, we have configured our JobTracker to use **FairScheduler**. With this scheduler, you can define a fixed set of job queues and allow specific users and groups to submit jobs to them. Each queue can also be configured with a custom list of administrators.

To enable the permissions model, you need to make some changes to your `mapred-site.xml` file:

```
<name>mapred.acls.enabled</name>
<value>true</value>
```

Next, you need to set the cluster level `mapred` administrators:

```
<name>mapred.cluster.administrators</name>
<value>alice,bob admin</value>
```

In the preceding examples, we have assigned administrator access to Linux users named `alice`, `bob` and to all the users in the admin Linux group. You can specify multiple users and groups with comma-separated lists. The users list must be separated from the group list with a space. The "*" symbol means everyone can perform administrative tasks on MapReduce jobs.

Very often, production Hadoop clusters execute jobs submitted by different groups within an organization. Such groups can have different priorities and their jobs can be of different importance. For example, there can be a production group whose jobs provide data for business critical applications and a analytics group performing background data mining. You can define which user can access which queue, as well as assign separate administrators for each queue.

First of all, you need to create a list of named queues in `mapred-site.xml`:

```
<name>mapred.queue.names</name>
<value>production,analytics</value>
```

Permissions for each job queue are defined in a separate file called `mapred-queue-acls.xml`. This file needs to be placed in the `/etc/hadoop/conf` directory on JobTracker. CDH provides a template file `mapred-queues.xml.template`, which you can use as a baseline.

The format of this file is a little bit different from the other Hadoop configuration files. The following is an example of what it may look like:

```
<queues>
 <queue>
   <name>production</name>
     <acl-submit-job> prodgroup</acl-submit-job>
     <acl-administer-jobs>alice </acl-administer-jobs>
 </queue>
 <queue>
   <name>analytics</name>
     <acl-submit-job> datascience</acl-submit-job>
     <acl-administer-jobs>bob </acl-administer-jobs>
 </queue>
</queues>
```

In the preceding example, we have defined two queues: `production` and `analytics`. Each queue supports a list of users and groups who can submit jobs to this queue, as well as the list of administrators. For the `production` group, we have limited submission rights only to the `prodgroup` Linux group using the `acl-submit-job` option. Note that there are no individual users listed and there is a leading space character before the group name. We have chosen `alice` as the production queue administrator and specified it using the `acl-administer-jobs` option. This particular configuration does not have a group in the list of administrators, and so a space character follows the username.

After you have made all the changes to `mapred-site.xml`, you need to restart the JobTracker service. Changes to `mapred-queue-acls.xml` are picked up automatically and no restart is required.

To submit a job to a given queue, you can use the `mapred.job.queue.name` option. For example, to submit a `WordCount` job into the analytics queue, you can use the following command:

```
# hadoop jar /usr/lib/hadoop-0.20-mapreduce/hadoop-examples.jar wordcount
-Dmapred.job.queue.name=analytics /tmp/word_in /tmp/word_out
```

You can monitor the list of active queues and jobs that are assigned to a particular queue by running the following `mapred` command:

```
# mapred queue -list
# mapred queue -info analytics -showJobs
```

Hadoop Service Level Authorization

In addition to the HDFS permissions model and MapReduce jobs queues administration, you can specify which users and groups can access the different cluster services. This can be useful to limit access to HDFS and submitting jobs only to a small set of users.

To enable service level authorization, you need to add the following option in the `core-site.xml` configuration file:

```
<name>hadoop.security.authorization</name>
<value>true</value>
```

Similarly, to MapReduce queue privileges, service level ACLs are defined in a separate file called `hadoop-policy.xml`. CDH provides a sample of this file in the `/etc/hadoop/conf` directory and, by default, it is wide open (all users can access all services).

The difference between Service Level Authorization and HDFS or MapReduce permissions is the order in which these checks are performed. Permissions checks on services' levels are performed before the user starts communicating with HDFS or the MapReduce service. This can be useful to block some users or groups from the cluster completely.

Let's say we want to limit the access of HDFS and MapReduce to only the Linux group named `hadoopusers`. To achieve this, we need to set the following options in `hadoop-policy.xml`:

```
<name>security.client.protocol.acl</name>
<value> hadoopusers</value>
<name>security.client.datanode.protocol.acl</name>
<value> hadoopusers</value>
```

The preceding options will prevent users other than those in the `hadoopusers` group from communicating with HDFS daemons. The format for the values is the same as we used for MapReduce permissions. Notice that there is a space character before "hadoopuser" string.

To allow only the members of the `hadoopuser` group to submit MapReduce jobs, specify the following option:

```
<name>security.job.submission.protocol.acl</name>
<value> hadoopusers</value>
```

There are many more possible options that you can specify in the `hadoop-policy.xml` file, basically limiting access to any Hadoop service, including internal communication protocols. For example, you could allow only the `hdfs` user to be used for inter-DataNode communication, as well as NameNode communication. All these options are outlined in the sample `hadoop-policy.xml` file, so you can tune them if necessary.

Hadoop and Kerberos

As you saw in the previous sections, Hadoop provides all the components to restrict access to various resources and services. There is still one piece of the puzzle missing, though. Since Hadoop doesn't maintain any internal user database, it has to completely trust users' identities as provided by the operating system. While Linux-based operating systems authenticate users with passwords or public/private key pairs, once a user is logged in, there is no way for Hadoop to correctly verify his/her identity. In the early versions of Hadoop, HDFS and MapReduce clients were executing an equivalent of the `whoami` shell command to get the identity of the user.

This was a very unsecure way of doing things, because it allowed a rogue user to just substitute the `whoami` command with a custom script that would return any username it liked.

In the latest version of Hadoop, code that retrieves the user identity was changed to use Java SecurityManager API, but the approach is still open to various security issues. One could change the client source code to use any identity and use this altered program to connect to the cluster. There are other possibilities of gaining unauthorized access to the cluster. An attacker might intercept and alter communication traffic between the client and Hadoop services, since it is not encrypted.

To address this problem, Hadoop supports authentication via an external Kerberos protocol. Kerberos is a protocol that was designed to allow participants to securely identify and authenticate themselves over an unsecure network. There are different implementations of this protocol available, but we will focus on **MIT Kerberos**.

Kerberos overview

Before we go over the steps required to implement Kerberos authentication with Hadoop, it is worth giving a brief overview of this protocol. Kerberos is a client-server protocol. It consists of **Key Distribution Center (KDC)**, as well as client programs.

KDC in its turn consists of several components. **Authentication Server (AS)** is responsible for verifying the user identity and issuing a **Ticket-Granting Ticket (TGT)**. AS has a local copy of the user's password and each TGT is encrypted with this password. When a client receives a TGT, it tries to decrypt it using password. If the password that the user provides and the one that AS stores match, then TGT can be successfully decrypted and used. Decrypted TGT is used to obtain an authentication ticket from **Ticket-Granting Service (TGS)**. This ticket is used to authenticate users against all the required services.

In Kerberos terminology, a user is called a **principal**. The principal consists of the following three components:

- **Primary component**: It is essentially a username.
- **Instance component**: It can be used to identify different roles for the same user, or to identify the same user on different servers in the Hadoop case.
- **Realm component**: It can be thought of as a domain in DNS.

Here is an example of a Kerberos principal:

```
alice/dn1.hadoop.test.com@HADOOP.TEST.COM
```

This is how the user `alice` connecting from one of the DataNodes will present herself to KDC.

Here is how the user would perform authentication with KDC and receive TGT:

```
[alice@dn1]$ kinit
Password for alice@HADOOP.TEST.COM:
...
```

The ticket obtained this way will be cached on the local filesystem and will be valid for the duration specified by the KDC administrator. Normally, this time frame is 8 to 12 hours, so users don't have to enter their passwords for every single operation. To be able to properly identify the realm, Kerberos client programs need to be installed on the server and the configuration needs to be provided in the `/etc/krb5.conf` file.

Kerberos in Hadoop

When Hadoop is configured with Kerberos support, all cluster interactions need to be first authenticated with KDC. This is valid, not only for cluster users, but for all Hadoop services as well. When Kerberos support is enabled, DataNode needs to have a proper ticket before it can communicate with NameNode.

This complicates the initial deployment, since you will need to generate principals for every service on every Hadoop node, as well as create principals for every cluster user. Since Hadoop services cannot interactively provide passwords, they use pregenerated keytab files, which are placed on each server.

After all principals are created and keytab files are distributed on all the servers, you will need to adjust the Hadoop configuration file to specify the principal and keytab file locations.

At this point, you should decide if implementing Kerberos on your cluster is required. Depending on the environment and type of data stored in the cluster, you may find that basic authentication provided by OS is enough in your case. If you have strict security requirements, implementing Kerberos support is the only solution available right now. Keep in mind that when enabled, Kerberos affects all the services in the cluster. It is not possible to implement partial support, let's say, for external users only.

Configuring Kerberos clients

We will not review the installation and configuration of KDC, since it's a vast topic in itself. We will assume that you have a dedicated MIT Kerberos Version 5 installed and configured, and you have KDC administrator account privileges.

The first task that you need to do is to install and configure the Kerberos client on all the servers. To install client programs, run the following command:

```
# yum install krb5-workstation.x86_64
```

After the client is installed, you need to edit the /etc/krb5.conf file and provide a Hadoop realm that was configured on KDC. We will use the HADOOP.TEST.COM realm in all the following examples. The name of the realm doesn't matter much in this case and you can choose a different one, if you'd like. In a production setup, you may want to use different realms for different clusters, such as production and QA.

Generating Kerberos principals

We will generate principals and keytab files for HDFS, MapReduce, and HTTP services. The HTTP principal is required to support built-in web services that are part of the HDFS and MapReduce daemons, and expose some status information to the users.

We will demonstrate how to generate these principals for one DataNode, because DataNodes will require HDFS, MapReduce, and HTTP principals to be specified. You will need to repeat this procedure for all the hosts in your cluster.

Automating principals generation

You can easily script commands to create Kerberos principals and generate keytab files and apply them to all servers. This will help you to avoid typos and mistakes.

Log in to the KDC server, switch to the root user, and execute the following commands:

```
# kadmin.local
Authenticating as principal root/admin@HADOOP.TEST.COM with password.
```

Some command-line output is omitted.

```
# kadmin.local
Authenticating as principal root/admin@HADOOP.TEST.COM with password.
addprinc -randkey HTTP/dn1.hadoop.test.com@HADOOP.TEST.COM
addprinc -randkey hdfs/dn1.hadoop.test.com@HADOOP.TEST.COM
addprinc -randkey mapred/dn1.hadoop.test.com@HADOOP.TEST.COM
```

The preceding commands will generate three principals with random passwords. We also need to generate keytab files for the hdfs and mapred principals. To do this, execute the following commands in the kadmin.local console:

```
xst -norandkey -k hdfs.keytab hdfs/dn1.hadoop.test.com@HADOOP.TEST.COM
HTTP/dn1.hadoop.test.com@HADOOP.TEST.COM
```

```
xst -norandkey -k mapred.keytab mapred/dn1.hadoop.test.com@HADOOP.TEST.
COM HTTP/dn1.hadoop.test.com@HADOOP.TEST.COM
```

The preceding commands will generate two files: hdfs.keytab and mapred.keytab. Copy these files to the appropriate server and place them in the /etc/hadoop/conf directory. To secure the keytab files, change the ownership of the files to hdfs:hdfs and mapred:mapred accordingly. Make sure that only these users are allowed to read the content of the file.

Before you move to the next step, you need to make sure that all the principals for all the nodes are generated and the keytab files are copied to all the servers.

Enabling Kerberos for HDFS

To enable Kerberos security, add the following option to the core-site.xml configuration file:

```
<name>hadoop.security.authentication</name>
<value>kerberos</value>
```

The default value for this variable is simple and it disables Kerberos support. Make sure you propagate changes in core-site.xml to all the servers in the cluster.

To configure Kerberos support for HDFS, you need to add the following options into the hdfs-site.xml file. It is important that this file is copied to all the HDFS servers in the cluster. Kerberos authentication is bi-directional. This means that DataNodes, for example, need to know the principal for the NameNode to communicate.

```
<name>dfs.block.access.token.enable</name>
<value>true</value>

<name>dfs.namenode.kerberos.principal</name>
<value>hdfs/_HOST@HADOOP.TEST.COM</value>

<name>dfs.datanode.kerberos.principal</name>
<value>hdfs/_HOST@HADOOP.TEST.COM</value>

<name>dfs.namenode.kerberos.internal.spnego.principal</name>
<value>HTTP/_HOST@HADOOP.TEST.COM</value>
```

```
<name>dfs.datanode.kerberos.http.principal</name>
<value>HTTP/_HOST@HADOOP.TEST.COM</value>

<name>dfs.journalnode.kerberos.principal</name>
<value>hdfs/_HOST@HADOOP.TEST.COM</value>

<name>dfs.journalnode.kerberos.internal.spnego.principal</name>
<value>HTTP/_HOST@HADOOP.TEST.COM</value>
```

The preceding options specify all HDFS related principals. Additionally, since we have configured NameNode High Availability, we have the specified principal for JournalNode as well. The _HOST token in these options will be replaced by a fully qualified hostname of the server at runtime.

Next, we need to provide the location of keytab files for HDFS principals:

```
<name>dfs.namenode.keytab.file</name>
<value>/etc/hadoop/conf/hdfs.keytab</value>

<name>dfs.datanode.keytab.file</name>
<value>/etc/hadoop/conf/hdfs.keytab</value>

<name>dfs.journalnode.keytab.file</name>
<value>/etc/hadoop/conf/hdfs.keytab</value>
```

One of the security requirements, not directly related to Kerberos, is to run DataNodes services on privileged ports. Privileged ports are ports with numbers below 1024. This is done to prevent a scenario when a rogue user writes a sophisticated MapReduce job that presents itself as a valid DataNode to the cluster. When security is enabled, you must make the following changes in the configuration file:

```
<name>dfs.datanode.address</name>
<value>0.0.0.0:1004</value>
<name>dfs.datanode.http.address</name>
<value>0.0.0.0:1006</value>
```

Finally, you need to create a /etc/default/hadoop-hdfs-datanode file with the following content:

```
export HADOOP_SECURE_DN_USER=hdfs
export HADOOP_SECURE_DN_PID_DIR=/var/lib/hadoop-hdfs
export HADOOP_SECURE_DN_LOG_DIR=/var/log/hadoop-hdfs
export JSVC_HOME=/usr/lib/bigtop-utils/
```

Enabling Kerberos for MapReduce

Changes that need to be applied to `mapred-site.xml` are very similar to what we have already done for HDFS. We need to provide principals and keytab file locations for JobTracker, TaskTrackers, and embedded web servers:

```
<name>mapreduce.jobtracker.kerberos.principal</name>
<value>mapred/_HOST@HADOOP.TEST.COM</value>

<name>mapreduce.jobtracker.kerberos.http.principal</name>
<value>mapred/_HOST@HADOOP.TEST.COM</value>

<name>mapreduce.tasktracker.kerberos.principal</name>
<value>HTTP/_HOST@HADOOP.TEST.COM</value>

<name>mapreduce.tasktracker.kerberos.http.principal</name>
<value>HTTP/_HOST@HADOOP.TEST.COM</value>

<name>mapreduce.jobtracker.keytab.file</name>
<value>/etc/hadoop/conf/mapred.keytab</value>

<name>mapreduce.tasktracker.keytab.file</name>
<value>/etc/hadoop/conf/mapred.keytab</value>
```

One thing that is specific to the MapReduce part of Hadoop when it comes to security is the fact that the user code is launched by TaskTracker in a separate JVM. This separate process, by default, is running under the user that started TaskTracker itself. This could potentially provide more permissions to the user that he or she needs. When security is enabled, TaskTracker changes the ownership of the process to a different user. This would be a user who launched the job. To support this, the following options need to be added:

```
<name>mapred.task.tracker.task-controller</name>
<value>org.apache.hadoop.mapred.LinuxTaskController</value>

<name>mapreduce.tasktracker.group</name>
<value>mapred</value>
```

Additionally, a separate `taskcontroller.cfg` file needs to be created in `/etc/hadoop/conf`. This file will specify the users who are allowed to launch tasks on this cluster. The following is the content of this file for our cluster:

```
mapred.local.dir=/dfs/data1/mapred,/dfs/data2/mapred,/dfs/data3/
mapred,/dfs/data4/mapred,/dfs/data5/mapred,/dfs/data6/mapred
hadoop.log.dir=/var/log/hadoop-0.20-mapreduce
```

```
mapreduce.tasktracker.group=mapred
banned.users=mapred,hdfs,bin
min.user.id=500
```

When running in secure mode, TaskTracker will launch different jobs under different users. We need to specify the locations of local directories in `taskcontroller.cfg` to allow TaskTracker to set permissions properly. We also specified users that are not allowed to execute MapReduce tasks using the `banned.users` option. This is required to avoid privileged users from bypassing security checks and accessing local data. The `min.user.id` option will disallow any of the privileged users with IDs of less than 500 (specific for CentOS) from submitting MapReduce jobs for the same reason.

After you have propagated these configuration files on all the nodes, you will need to restart all the services in the cluster. Pay close attention to the messages in the logfiles. As you can see, configuring a secure Hadoop cluster is not a simple task, with a lot of steps involved. It is important to double check that all the services are working properly.

Summary

In this chapter, we have reviewed the authentication and authorization principles used in Hadoop. We have discussed the HDFS permissions model, as well as MapReduce access control lists. The default Hadoop security policy is prone to various attacks. We have reviewed how to configure Kerberos support in Hadoop to comply with enterprise-level security requirements.

In the next chapter, we will focus on monitoring Hadoop cluster's health and performance.

5
Monitoring Hadoop Cluster

Every production system requires a well-planned monitoring strategy; hence Hadoop cluster also requires it. It is not a simple task, taking into account the multiple components involved and the multiple machines comprising of the cluster. Hadoop provides a wide variety of metrics about the internal state of its components, but there are no ready to use tools to monitor and alert on these metrics. In this chapter, we will provide an overview of the monitoring strategy, as well as tools that you can use to implement it.

Monitoring strategy overview

Hadoop monitoring strategy is different from what you may use for traditional databases.When you have a cluster of hundreds of servers, failure of various components becomes a norm. If you will treat a failure of single DataNode as an emergency, there is a big chance that your monitoring system will be overloaded with false alerts.

Instead, it is important to outline which components are critical and failure of which components can be tolerated (up to a certain point). For critical components, you will need to define rules, which will alert on call personnel right away. For non-critical components, regular reports on the overall system status should be enough.

You should already have an idea about Hadoop components whose failure should be treated as an emergency. Failure of NameNode or a JobTracker will make cluster unusable and should be investigated right away. Even if you have High Availability configured for these components, it is still important to find out what was the root cause of the problem. This will help you to prevent similar problems occurring in the future. If you have followed our instructions to set up High Availability for the NameNode with automatic failover, it is important to provide proper monitoring for all the involved components.

You need to make sure that enough JournalNodes are up and running to provide **quorum** for NameNode logs, as well as monitor the ZooKeeper cluster status. Besides complete failures of a given service, you will also need to monitor some health metrics to be able to prevent disasters. Things such as available disk space on NameNode and JournalNodes, as well as total cluster capacity and current usage are one of the most critical metrics that you should monitor.

Worker nodes are the non-critical part of the cluster from a monitoring perspective. Hadoop can tolerate failure of several worker nodes and still keep the cluster available. It is important to monitor what portion of DataNodes and TaskTrackers is available, and configure monitoring rules based on this metric. For example, failure of one or two worker nodes may not need immediate attention from the Operations team. Failure of 30 percent of the worker nodes on the other hand compromises cluster availability and is probably a sign of a larger problem. It could be caused by a faulty hardware or network outage.

Hadoop doesn't come with any built-in monitoring system. The most common practice is the use of open source monitoring systems such as Nagios for alerting, and tools such as Ganglia for trending and historical information. In the following sections, we will review the metrics Hadoop services reveals and how to access them. We will also look at how to integrate these metrics with the existing monitoring systems.

Hadoop Metrics

Most of the Hadoop components reveal the status of their internal components via a metrics subsystem. The idea is to keep counters specific to a given Hadoop process and redirect them according to the configuration to a proper consumer.

The Hadoop Metrics subsystem has several versions. The older one is called metrics1 (or just metrics), and the newer one is referred to as metrics2. Metrics2 is available starting CHD4 and we will focus on this version.

Metrics2 has a notion of sources, sinks, and contexts. A **source** is any component that records internal statistics, such as NameNode or JobTracker. Sources collect metrics in various **contexts**. For example, NameNode can reveal information about the JVM it is running in via jvm context, information about the HDFS state via dfs context, and information about RPC via rpc context. **Sink** is a consumer for metrics. A sink can be a text file, a file for a specific monitoring system, and so on.

By default, Hadoop components collect metrics, but do not provide them to any consumers. To enable particular sinks, you need to edit the `hadoop-metrics2.properties` file. You can also notice that there is a `hadoop-metrics.properties` file in `/etc/hadoop/conf`. This one is used by the earlier versions of a metrics subsystem. We will focus on metrics2, though.

There are several options that are enabled in the metrics2 configuration file, by default:

```
*.sink.file.class=org.apache.hadoop.metrics2.sink.FileSink
*.period=10
```

These configuration options enable a file sink, basically meaning that configured sources will just write their output to a text file. Metrics will be sampled every 10 seconds in this case.

For example, to configure NameNode statistics to be written out to a file, you should add the following line to the `hadoop-metrics2.properties` file:

```
namenode.sink.file.filename=/var/log/hadoop-hdfs/namenode-metrics.out
```

You need to restart Hadoop daemons to apply these changes.

In general, you will not need to configure writing out metrics to plain text files, unless you plan to develop a custom script to process them. Instead, we will use metrics that Hadoop services reveal through Java Management Extensions (JMX).

JMX Metrics

Most Hadoop components implement JMX interfaces to reveal some information about their internal status. This data can be explored using tools such as JConsole (`http://docs.oracle.com/javase/6/docs/technotes/guides/management/jconsole.html`), but we will focus on another way to obtain these metrics—through the HTTP interface.

Core Hadoop components have an embedded web server, which is used to provide some user-friendly status information about the service. For example, to see the NameNode status page, go to the following URL—`http://nn1.hadoop.test.com:50070`. Different services use different default ports and the table below provides a brief summary:

Service name	HTTP port
NameNode	50070
DataNode	50075
JournalNode	8480

Service name	HTTP port
JobTracker	50030
TaskTracker	50060

Besides general status information, Hadoop services also expose JMX metrics on /jmx page. For example, to get DataNode metrics, go to `http://dn1.hadoop.test.com:50075/jmx`. These metrics are similar to what you would see if you stream them to a text file, but are provided in a JSON format. JSON is not only more readable, but is easier to parse in various scripts.

Metrics exposed on /jmx page are organized in separate contexts. There are quite a few of them and the total number of metrics is intimidating. We will, however, focus only on the several most important metrics for our monitoring purposes.

Here is an example of the `FSNamesystem` context fetched from active NameNode (not all metrics are shown here):

```
{
    "name" : "Hadoop:service=NameNode,name=FSNamesystem",
    "tag.Hostname" : "nn2.hadoop.test.com",
    "MissingBlocks" : 0,
    "CapacityTotalGB" : 62.0,
    "CapacityUsedGB" : 0.0,
    "CapacityRemainingGB" : 48.0,
    "BlocksTotal" : 19,
    "FilesTotal" : 44,
    "PendingReplicationBlocks" : 0,
    "UnderReplicatedBlocks" : 19,
    "CorruptBlocks" : 0,
    "BlockCapacity" : 2097152,
    "TotalFiles" : 44
}
```

As you can see, JMX exposes some critical information about the HDFS status, such as remaining disk space, corrupted and under replicated blocks. We will rely on this information to build our monitoring solution.

Monitoring Hadoop with Nagios

There are several ways that you can implement operational monitoring of a Hadoop cluster. Hadoop distributions vendors such as Cloudera, MapR, and Hortonworks provide their own cluster monitoring and management software. In most cases, this software, or some of its features are available only with a paid subscription.

If you are planning to purchase support from one of these vendors, it is worth looking into features provided by their monitoring systems.

Another option, is to use a freely available monitoring framework, such as Nagios. Nagios checks are pluggable, and you can define alerting rules based on any metric that is available to you. Nagios is one of the most popular open source monitoring systems, and it is quite possible that you are already using it to monitor the components of your IT infrastructure. If not, please refer to the Nagios documentation for installation and configuration details at `http://www.nagios.org/documentation`.

Monitoring HDFS

We can classify our monitoring checks as host-specific and Hadoop-specific, as well as critical and non-critical. Host-specific checks would include things that you would normally check on any Linux server: disk space, memory usage, and so on. Hadoop specific checks will be based on the metrics provided by Hadoop services. An example of a critical event would be complete JobTracker failure. In this case, an on call member of the Operations team should investigate and address the problem right away. Non-critical checks can be regarded as daily reports on the cluster status. An example of one such report could be a percentage of available DataNode servers.

NameNode checks

The following OS and host-level checks should be configured on the NameNode servers:

- Check if the server is reachable. This can be easily implemented using the `check_ping` plugin from the Nagios plugins package available at `http://nagiosplugins.org/`. If you are using HA setup for NameNode, it is important to check both, primary and secondary, NameNodes. Type: critical

- Check the disk space available for both NameNode filesystem and edit logs directories as well as for OS volume. You can use `check_disk` from Nagios plugins for this purpose. Nagios allows you to configure different levels of alerts. You can configure it to enter the WARNING state when check results cross one threshold, and the CRITICAL state when another threshold is reached. Type: critical

- It is important to make sure the NameNode service doesn't swap. Swapping can significantly increase the response time for RPC calls and effectively stall the cluster. There is a `check_swap` plugin available to do this. Type: critical

- Monitor any hardware failure alerts, especially RAID health. There are various vendor-specific checks available as Nagios plugins on `http://exchange.nagios.org/directory/Plugins/Hardware/Storage-Systems/RAID-Controllers`. Type: critical

In general, host level monitoring can be implemented in the same way as you currently monitor other Linux servers. Implementing Hadoop-specific checks is less straightforward. There are no ready-to-use implementations for different Hadoop metrics. There are several open source scripts on the Internet that parse the content of the JMX web page and alert on different metrics. These scripts are not generic enough to allow you to monitor all things that you may want though.

Since we are focusing on JMX web output, which is provided in a JSON format, it is easy to write a script using the language of your choice to parse it and extract the information that you are interested in. We will not focus on implementation specifics of such scripts, since they will be different for different languages. Instead, we will list what JMX metrics should be monitored.

The following list describes Hadoop-specific checks that should be monitored on a production cluster:

Service level checks are checks that are specific to Hadoop processes. Let's take a look at what checks can be implemented for HDFS:

- You can monitor the available HDFS capacity by looking at the `CapacityTotalGB/CapacityUsedGB/CapacityRemainingGB` status variable in the NameNode JMX output. Monitoring HDFS capacity should be done on both, alerting level and regular reporting level as well. You need to know the long-term disk space consumption rate to be able to perform proper capacity planning. It is also important to have an alerting check for these metrics to prevent a situation where a runaway user job consumes all the cluster disk space. Type: critical and regular
- If you are storing lots of smaller files, there is a chance you can run out of available block slots on NameNode before you actually run out of disk space. To avoid this, you need to monitor `BlocksTotal` and `BlockCapacity` status variables. Type: critical and regular
- If there is a block whose replicas are all corrupted, it is marked as a corrupted block. The total amount of such blocks in the cluster is reported in the `CorruptedBlocks` variable. There is no fixed threshold to monitor, but ideally this number should be close to 0. Type: critical
- The number of blocks that do not have any replicas available is reported in the `MissingBlocks` status variable. As in the previous case, this number should be very low. Type: critical

- It is important to monitor the percentage of available DataNodes in the cluster. This can be done by looking at the `NumLiveDataNodes` and `NumDeadDataNodes` status variables. Depending on your cluster size, you can either alert on a fixed number of dead DataNodes or on the ratio of alive to dead nodes. For example, you could set up a rule to alert you when there are more than three failed nodes. Another approach is to alert when less than 70 percent of nodes are alive. It is a good idea to have both regular and alerting checks setup for this. Type: critical and regular
- When we configured NameNode, we have specified what is the maximum amount of memory this process can consume. To monitor the status of memory usage, you need to look at `HeapMemoryUsage.max` and `HeapMemoryUsage.used` status variables. If the memory used will exceed the maximum NameNode memory limit, the process will crash with an "out of memory" error. Monitoring these variables is trickier, because the value of `HeapMemoryUsage.used` can go up and down as garbage collection happens. You may need to monitor the average value over some period of time to get an accurate idea about the current memory usage. Type: critical

JournalNode checks

JournalNode is a service specific to NameNode HA implementation. There are not that many service specific metrics that are critical to monitor. You need to make sure the JournalNode process is running, it's not going to run out of memory or disk space, and so on. Since JournalNodes are often collocated with other services, you don't need to duplicate host-level checks that already exist.

The following is a list of host-level resources to monitor on a JournalNode:

- Check if the server is reachable using ping. Type: critical
- Check disk space on editlog volume. Type: critical
- Check swap usage on the server. Type: critical

The following checks are specific to a JournalNode process:

- **Make sure service is running**: This can be done by either monitoring the process from an OS perspective, or making sure the JMX metrics page returns the expected results. Type: critical
- **Monitor memory usage**: Like in the case with NameNode, the status variables that you need to look at are `HeapMemoryUsage.used` and `HeapMemoryUsage.max`. Type: critical

ZooKeeper checks

- ZooKeeper is a standalone project that is used in Hadoop deployments for various purposes. One of the reasons we used it in our setup is to support the failover procedures with NameNode HA. Without keeping a track of which NameNode is primary and which is secondary, there could be situations where both nodes will try to update the filesystem state causing corruption.

- ZooKeeper is a distributed system, which is designed to tolerate failure of several nodes. It is critical to monitor how many nodes in ZooKeeper cluster are alive at any given moment.

> If you want your ZooKeeper cluster to tolerate failure of N machines, you need to configure 2 * N + 1 servers.

- Unfortunately, ZooKeeper doesn't provide a similar HTTP interface to its internal metrics. Instead, you can connect to the service port using tools such as telnet, and execute specific commands that will print out service status metrics:

```
# telnet localhost 2181
Trying ::1...
Connected to localhost.
Escape character is '^]'.
mntr
zk_version  3.4.5-cdh4.3.0--1, built on 05/28/2013 02:01 GMT
zk_avg_latency  0
zk_max_latency  196
zk_min_latency  0
zk_packets_received  28099
zk_packets_sent  28097
zk_num_alive_connections  1
zk_outstanding_requests  0
zk_server_state  leader
zk_znode_count  10
zk_watch_count  0
zk_ephemerals_count  1
zk_approximate_data_size  365
zk_open_file_descriptor_count  30
zk_max_file_descriptor_count  1024
zk_followers  2
zk_synced_followers  2
zk_pending_syncs  0
```

The `mntr` command is one of the commands that ZooKeeper understands, and it basically shows you the service status. If you are connected to the cluster leader, you will see the number of active followers by looking at the `zk_synced_followers` line. If this metric goes below the ZooKeeper redundancy threshold, an alert should be triggered.

If you are using dedicated ZooKeeper servers, you will need to implement basic host-level checks as well.

Monitoring MapReduce

When it comes to monitoring the MapReduce status in the current Hadoop implementation, all required metrics can be obtained on the JobTracker level. There is no reason to monitor individual TaskTrackers, at least on an alert level. A periodic report on the number of alive and dead TaskTrackers should be sent out to monitor the overall framework health.

JobTracker checks

The following is the list of host-level resources to monitor on a JobTracker:

- Check if the server is reachable using ping. Type: critical
- Check disk space on logs and system volumes. JobTracker doesn't preserve state on a local filesystem, but not being able to write to the log files due to low disk space will cause issues. Type: critical
- Check swap usage on the server. Type: critical

The following checks are specific to JobTracker process::

- Monitor memory usage. You can monitor JobTracker memory usage by checking `HeapMemoryUsage.used` and `HeapMemoryUsage.max` variables. Type: critical
- Checking the `SummaryJson.nodes` and `SummaryJson.alive` status variables will give you an idea of what portion of TaskTrackers is available at any given moment in time. There is no strict threshold for this metric. Your jobs will run even if there is only one TaskTracker available, but performance will, obviously, deteriorate significantly. Choose a threshold based on your cluster size, and adjust it over time according to what the failure trend is. Type: critical

JobTracker can blacklist some of the worker nodes if they constantly report slow performance or fail too often. You should monitor the total number of blacklisted TaskTrackers by looking at the `SummaryJson.blacklisted` metric. Type: critical

Monitoring Hadoop with Ganglia

While Nagios, or any other operational monitoring system will alert if things go wrong, it is also very useful to be able to graph various cluster metrics and explore trends. **Ganglia** is an open source package that was designed specifically to monitor large clusters. It provides access to the data via the web interface, can aggregate metrics across multiple machines, and so on.

To enable Hadoop metrics that are sent to Ganglia stats collection daemons, you need to add the following options in `/etc/hadoop/conf/Hadoop-metrics2.properties`:

```
*.sink.ganglia.class=org.apache.hadoop.metrics2.sink.ganglia.
GangliaSink31
*.sink.ganglia.period=10
*.sink.ganglia.supportsparse=true
*.sink.ganglia.slope=jvm.metrics.gcCount=zero,jvm.metrics.
memHeapUsedM=both
*.sink.ganglia.dmax=jvm.metrics.threadsBlocked=70,jvm
```

Additionally, you will need to point all sinks to your Ganglia collector server:

```
namenode.sink.ganglia.servers=gangliahost:8649
datanode.sink.ganglia.servers=gangliahost:8649
jobtracker.sink.ganglia.servers=gangliahost:8649
tasktracker.sink.ganglia.servers=gangliahost:8649
maptask.sink.ganglia.servers=gangliahost:8649
reducetask.sink.ganglia.servers=gangliahost:8649
```

Summary

Hadoop doesn't provide any out of the box monitoring capabilities, but it does reveal lots of information about the internal status of its components. You can use the existing open source tools to monitor these metrics, and alert you when critical events happen. Unlike a traditional database system, not every component failure should be treated with the same priority and you should keep this in mind when implementing a monitoring solution. Separating checks into critical and regular groups would allow you to monitor the Hadoop cluster with a decent degree of flexibility.

Until now, we were discussing how to build and host your own Hadoop cluster. There are many use cases where owning and maintaining the full Hadoop infrastructure is not the best choice. An alternative to this approach is using a cloud infrastructure. In the next chapter, we will review the options you have if you want to host your cluster in the cloud.

6

Deploying Hadoop to the Cloud

Previously, we were focused on deploying Hadoop on real physical servers. This is the most common and generally recommended way to use Hadoop. The Hadoop cluster performs the best when it can fully utilize the available hardware resources. Previously, using virtualized servers for Hadoop was not considered a good practice. This has been changing over the past few years. More and more people realized that the main benefit of running Hadoop in the cloud is not the performance, but rather the great flexibility when it comes to provisioning resources. With cloud you can create large clusters of hundreds of computer nodes in no time, perform the required task, and then destroy the cluster if you don't need it any longer. In this chapter, we will describe the several options you have when deploying Hadoop in the cloud. We will focus on **Amazon Web Services (AWS)** since it is the most popular public cloud at the moment, and it also provides some advanced features for Hadoop.

Amazon Elastic MapReduce

AWS is probably one of the most popular public clouds at the moment. It allows users to quickly provision virtual servers on demand and discard them when they are no longer required. While Hadoop was not originally designed to run in such environments, the ability to create large clusters for specific tasks is very appealing in many use cases.

Imagine you need to process application logfiles and prepare data to be loaded in relational databases. If this task takes a couple of hours and runs only once a day, there is little reason to keep the Hadoop cluster running all the time, as it would be idle most of the time. In this case, a more practical solution would be to provision a virtual cluster using **Elastic MapReduce (EMR)** and destroy it after the work is done.

EMR clusters don't have to be destroyed and recreated from scratch every time. You can choose to keep the cluster running and use it for interactive Hive queries, and so on.

We will now take you through the steps to provision a Hadoop cluster using EMR. We will assume that you are familiar with the main AWS concepts such as EC2, instance types, regions, and so on. You can always refer to the AWS documentation for more details at the following website:

`https://aws.amazon.com/documentation/`

Installing the EMR command-line interface

You can interact with EMR in different ways. AWS provides a great web console interface for all its services. This means that you don't have to use a command line to create, launch, and monitor clusters. This may be fine for testing end exploring, but when it's time to implement an EMR job as part of the production ETL process, the command line comes in handy.

Though this is a high-level overview of EMR capabilities, we will focus on using a command line instead of a web interface, because this is what you will do in a production environment.

To install the EMR Command-line Interface (CLI), you need to perform the following steps:

1. Download CLI and unpack the tools from the website.

    `http://aws.amazon.com/developertools/2264.`

2. Depending on your platform, you may need to install Ruby.

3. Create an S3 bucket to store the logfiles produced by Hadoop. Since, in many cases, temporary EMR clusters are running unattended, you need a persistent location for the logfiles to be able to review the status or debug issues.

4. To be able to use EMR CLI, you need to have your AWS Access Key ID ready and also generate a key pair. You should refer to the AWS documentation for details on how to obtain your Access Key at `http://docs.aws.amazon.com/general/latest/gr/getting-aws-sec-creds.html`.

5. You need to change the permissions on the key pair `.pem` file to be only readable by the owner: `chmod og-rwx emr-keys.pem`.

6. Now, you can create a configuration for EMR CLI. Go to the directory where you have placed the CLI files and edit the `credentials.json` file to look like this:

```
{
"access_id": "Your Access Key ID",
"private_key": "Your AWS Secret Access Key",
"keypair": "emr-keys",
"key-pair-file": "/path/to/key-file/emr-keys.pem",
"log_uri": "s3n://emr-logs-x123/",
"egion": "us-east-1"
}
```

This sample configuration file has all the options you need to launch the test EMR cluster. To verify that CLI works properly, just run it with the -version option:

```
# ./elastic-mapreduce --version
Version 2013-07-08
```

You can refer to the EMR CLI documentation for more details at `http://docs.aws.amazon.com/ElasticMapReduce/latest/DeveloperGuide/emr-cli-install.html`.

Choosing the Hadoop version

EMR makes launching Hadoop clusters easy by taking care of deploying and configuring Hadoop components. You don't have to manually download, install, and configure packages. On the other hand, EMR provides a decent amount of flexibility. You can control different aspects of your cluster configuration by passing parameters to `elastic-mapreduce` CLI. One of the options you can specify is which Hadoop version to use. To do this, you need to pass the -hadoop-version option to CLI. Currently, EMR supports the following Hadoop versions: 1.0.3, 0.20.205, 0.20, and 0.18. If you don't specify the Hadoop version explicitly, the EMR cluster will be launched using the latest Hadoop version.

Launching the EMR cluster

Once you have installed and configured CLI tools, launching a new EMR cluster is very easy. The following command will start a 3-node Hadoop cluster:

```
# ./elastic-mapreduce --create --alive --name "EMR Test" \
--num-instances 3 --instance-type m1.small
Created job flow j-2RNNYC3TUCZIO
```

There are several important options to this command. The `--alive` option tells EMR to launch the cluster and make it available for the user to connect to servers via SSH and perform any tasks that they may need to. An alternative to this approach is to launch a cluster to execute one specified job and automatically terminate the cluster when it is completed. We will explore this option in more detail later. We have also specified the name of the cluster, how many servers to launch, and what type of EC2 instances to use.

This command will be executed almost instantly, but it doesn't mean your cluster is ready to use right away. It may take EMR several minutes to launch the cluster. EMR uses the term job flow to describe clusters. The idea behind this is that you can set up a number of steps such as launch the cluster, run the Hive script, save data, and terminate the cluster. These steps form a job flow and can be executed automatically. In this case, CLI prints out the ID of the cluster that we have started. Since it takes some time to launch the cluster, you can use the `--describe` option to check the current status:

```
# ./elastic-mapreduce --jobflow j-2RNNYC3TUCZIO --describe
```

The preceding command provides a lot of useful information about your cluster. The output is a JSON document, which makes it easy to be consumed by various automation scripts. We will take a look at the first section that shows the current status of the cluster:

```
"ExecutionStatusDetail": {
        "CreationDateTime": 1375748997.0,
        "ReadyDateTime": null,
        "EndDateTime": null,
        "StartDateTime": null,
        "State": "STARTING",
        "LastStateChangeReason": "Starting instances"
    }
```

You can see that the `State` field has the `STARTING` status, which means that the cluster is not yet ready to be used. If you re-run this command in a couple of minutes, you should see `State` changing to `WAITING`. This means you can connect to your cluster and start executing jobs.

Once the EMR cluster is in the `WAITING` state, you can identify your master instance by looking at the `MasterPublicDnsName` field:

```
"Instances": {
        "SlaveInstanceType": "m1.small",
        "HadoopVersion": "1.0.3",
        "Ec2KeyName": "emr-keys",
```

```
        "MasterPublicDnsName": "ec2-107-20-83-146.compute-1.amazonaws.
com",

        "TerminationProtected": false,
        "NormalizedInstanceHours": 3,
        "MasterInstanceType": "m1.small",
        "KeepJobFlowAliveWhenNoSteps": true,
        "Ec2SubnetId": null,
        "Placement": {
          "AvailabilityZone": "us-east-1a"
        }
```

Master instance in EMR clusters is the instance that is hosting Hadoop NameNode and JobTracker. It is also your gateway to access the cluster. You can log in to the master instance using the key pair that you generated earlier when configuring CLI tools.

> Another way to check the cluster status and get the address of the master instance is by using the EMR Web console available at
> https://console.aws.amazon.com/elasticmapreduce/home?region=us-east-1

You can terminate the EMR cluster once you no longer need it:

```
# ./elastic-mapreduce --jobflow j-2RNNYC3TUCZIO --terminate
Terminated job flow j-2RNNYC3TUCZIO
```

Temporary EMR clusters

Another way to use EMR is to launch a temporary cluster. In this case, you need to prepare input and output data locations, as well as a .jar file with a MapReduce job or the Hadoop streaming script. Once this is done, you can launch the EMR cluster that will process the data (that you provide using your MapReduce job), write the output into the specified location, and terminate the cluster when the work is done. This approach doesn't require any human interaction (once you prepared input data and MapReduce job) and can be easily scheduled to run on a regular basis.

Preparing input and output locations

One thing to keep in mind with temporary EMR clusters is that the HDFS storage is temporary as well. This means that you can use HDFS while the cluster is running, but the data will be deleted when the EMR cluster is terminated. EMR solves this problem by relying on the Amazon S3 storage service. You can specify S3 buckets as input and output sources for EMR clusters.

Before you can launch your EMR cluster, you need to create the S3 buckets that will be used to store the input/output data for your cluster. Depending on your preferences, you can use the AWS web console to create buckets or use AWS command line tools. You can refer to the S3 documentation for more details at

http://aws.amazon.com/documentation/s3/

For our test, we will create two buckets: emr-logs-x123 and emr-data-x123.

> In the S3 bucket, the name must be globally unique. You may need to adjust your bucket names to satisfy this rule.

We will use the emr-data-x123 bucket to store input and output data, as well as store the .jar file for our MapReduce job. You will need to create the input directory for the input data and the jobs directory for the .jar files. The simplest way to create directories in S3 buckets is via the S3 web interface. You can also upload a sample text file into the input directory using the same interface.

EMR relies on S3, not only to store input and output data, but also to keep MapReduce programs. You can place the .jar files or streaming scripts on S3 and point your EMR cluster to it. In this example, we will use the WordCount program that comes with the Hadoop distribution. We will create the mapreduce-jobs directory in the same emr-data-x123 bucket and place the hadoop-examples-1.0.3.jar file there.

> The hadoop-examples.jar file is supplied with all Hadoop distributions. You need to make sure the version of this file matches the version of the EMR cluster you are planning to launch.

We will use the emr-logs-x123 S3 bucket to keep the logfiles of the EMR job attempts. You can always refer to these files to get additional information about your job.

Once you have completed all the preparation steps, you can use EMR CLI to launch the cluster and execute the job:

```
# ./elastic-mapreduce --create --name "Word Count JAR Test" \
  --jar s3n://emr-data-x123/mapreduce-jobs/hadoop-examples-1.0.3.jar \
  --arg wordcount \
  --arg s3n://emr-data-x123/input/cont-test.txt \
  --arg s3n://emr-tests-x123/output/
```

The arguments to the preceding command are very similar to what you would use for running a MapReduce job on a standard Hadoop cluster. We specify the location of the .jar file on S3, the name of the class to execute, as well as locations of the input and output data directories. The location of the S3 bucket for logfiles is not specified here, but is a part of the credentials.json configuration files described previously in *Installing the EMR command-line interface* section..

Once the job is completed, the EMR cluster will be terminated automatically, but S3 directories will still be available.

 You can get more details of EMR and S3 specifics at http://docs. aws.amazon.com/ElasticMapReduce/latest/DeveloperGuide/ emr-plan-file-systems.html

Using Whirr

Using EMR is not the only way to deploy Hadoop in the cloud. If you prefer more control over the cluster installation and configuration process, you may want to explore other options.

Whirr is an Apache project that was developed to automate setting up and configuring Hadoop clusters in the cloud. Unlike EMR, Whirr can create Hadoop clusters using not only Amazon EC2, but also other cloud providers. As of now, Whirr supports EC2 and Rackspace cloud.

Installing and configuring Whirr

Whirr is not another Hadoop component. It is a collection of Java programs that helps you to automate creating a Hadoop cluster in the cloud. You can download Whirr from the project's website at:

http://www.apache.org/dyn/closer.cgi/whirr/

Whirr doesn't require any special steps to be installed. You can download the archive, unpack it, and start using the whirr binary, which can be found in the bin directory.

There are several configuration files you need to tune before you can use Whirr to launch clusters:

1. First of all, you need to create the ~/.whirr/credentials file in your home directory. This file contains credentials that will be used to provision instances using your cloud provider. In case of Amazon EC2, this will be your Access Key ID and Secret Access Key. If you are using the Rackspace cloud, you will need to provide the username and API Key. You will have to copy the template file from conf/credentials.sample located in the Whirr installation directory.

2. Next, you need to create a configuration file for your cluster. Here is a sample test-hadoop.properties file:

```
whirr.cluster-name=testhadoop
whirr.instance-templates=1 hadoop-jobtracker 1 hadoop-namenode,5
hadoop-datanode+hadoop-tasktracker
whirr.provider=aws-ec2
whirr.private-key-file=${sys:user.home}/.ssh/id_rsa
whirr.public-key-file=${sys:user.home}/.ssh/id_rsa.pub
```

3. This configuration defines a 7-node cluster using Amazon EC2. The way Whirr specifies a cluster layout is very simple; you just need to specify the number and types of instances you want in the whirr-instance-templates variable. You will also need to generate a dedicated key pair to be used for the cluster setup. To launch the cluster with this configuration, run:

```
#whirr launch-cluster --config test-hadoop.properties
```

4. When you are done with the cluster, you can easily decommission it by running:

```
#whirr destroy-cluster --config test-hadoop.properties
```

For more information on the available Whirr options, please refer to the project's documentation page at

```
http://whirr.apache.org/docs/0.8.1/configuration-guide.html#cloud-
provider-config
```

Summary

In this chapter, we have reviewed ways to create Hadoop clusters on demand by using the Elastic MapReduce service from AWS, as well as Apache Whirr. Running Hadoop in a cloud allows users to launch large clusters for short periods of time to process massive amounts of data. You don't have to maintain your own Hadoop infrastructure and most of the cluster configuration steps are automated.

Index

configuration files 104
installing 103

Y

yum command 30
yum package
  setting up 26

Z

ZooKeeper
  about 28, 31
  service, starting 32
ZooKeeper checks 94
zookeeper package 30

Thank you for buying
Hadoop Cluster Deployment

About Packt Publishing

Packt, pronounced 'packed', published its first book "*Mastering phpMyAdmin for Effective MySQL Management*" in April 2004 and subsequently continued to specialize in publishing highly focused books on specific technologies and solutions.

Our books and publications share the experiences of your fellow IT professionals in adapting and customizing today's systems, applications, and frameworks. Our solution based books give you the knowledge and power to customize the software and technologies you're using to get the job done. Packt books are more specific and less general than the IT books you have seen in the past. Our unique business model allows us to bring you more focused information, giving you more of what you need to know, and less of what you don't.

Packt is a modern, yet unique publishing company, which focuses on producing quality, cutting-edge books for communities of developers, administrators, and newbies alike. For more information, please visit our website: www.packtpub.com.

About Packt Open Source

In 2010, Packt launched two new brands, Packt Open Source and Packt Enterprise, in order to continue its focus on specialization. This book is part of the Packt Open Source brand, home to books published on software built around Open Source licences, and offering information to anybody from advanced developers to budding web designers. The Open Source brand also runs Packt's Open Source Royalty Scheme, by which Packt gives a royalty to each Open Source project about whose software a book is sold.

Writing for Packt

We welcome all inquiries from people who are interested in authoring. Book proposals should be sent to author@packtpub.com. If your book idea is still at an early stage and you would like to discuss it first before writing a formal book proposal, contact us; one of our commissioning editors will get in touch with you.

We're not just looking for published authors; if you have strong technical skills but no writing experience, our experienced editors can help you develop a writing career, or simply get some additional reward for your expertise.

Hadoop Operations and Cluster Management Cookbook

ISBN: 978-1-78216-516-3   Paperback: 368 pages

Over 60 recipes showing you how to design, configure, manage, monitor, and tune a Hadoop cluster

1. Hands-on recipes to configure a Hadoop cluster from bare metal hardware nodes

2. Practical and in depth explanation of cluster management commands

3. Easy-to-understand recipes for securing and monitoring a Hadoop cluster, and design considerations

Securing Hadoop

ISBN: 978-1-78328-525-9   Paperback: 98 pages

Implement a robust end-to-end security for your Hadoop ecosystem

1. Master the key concepts behind Hadoop security as well as how to secure a Hadoop-based Big Data ecosystem

2. Understand and deploy authentication, authorization, and data encryption in a Hadoop-based Big Data platform

3. Administer the auditing and security event monitoring system

Please check **www.PacktPub.com** for information on our titles

Hadoop Beginner's Guide

ISBN: 978-1-84951-730-0   Paperback: 398 pages

Learn how to crunch big data to extract meaning from the data avalanche

1. Learn tools and techniques that let you approach big data with relish and not fear

2. Shows how to build a complete infrastructure to handle your needs as your data grows

3. Hands-on examples in each chapter give the big picture while also giving direct experience

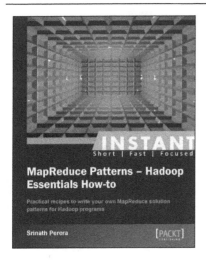

Instant MapReduce Patterns – Hadoop Essentials How-to

ISBN: 978-1-78216-770-9   Paperback: 60 pages

Practical recipes to write your own MapReduce solution patterns for Hadoop programs

1. Learn something new in an Instant! A short, fast, focused guide delivering immediate results.

2. Learn how to install, configure, and run Hadoop jobs.

3. Seven recipes, each describing a particular style of the MapReduce program to give you a good understanding of how to program with MapReduce.

Please check **www.PacktPub.com** for information on our titles

www.ingramcontent.com/pod-product-compliance
Lightning Source LLC
Chambersburg PA
CBHW060154060326
40690CB00018B/4111